Frank M. Ahearn
The Digital Hit Man
His Weapons for Combating the Digital World

International Skip Tracer and Privacy Expert Frank M. Ahearn has located people hiding in all parts of the globe as well as successfully "disappeared" those who did not want to be found. At present, he is the number one expert specializing in digital deception in order to combat digital intrusion which is the fastest growing problem among citizens who are concerned about their personal privacy. He is co-author of the bestselling book *How to Disappear: Erase Your Digital Footprint, Leave False Trails, and Vanish without a Trace* which has been published in over ten countries.

Frank M. Ahearn is a native New Yorker and divides his time between, New York, Venice Beach and Paris France.

Frank M. Ahearn
The Digital Hit Man
His Weapons for Combating the Digital World

By
Frank M. Ahearn

Published by LYING.FR
163 Amsterdam Ave #172
New York, NY 10023
www.FrankAhearn.com
ISBN 978-0-615-59583-2

CONTACT
www.Frankahearn.com
Lying.FR

Library of Congress Cataloging-in-Publication Data is available on file.

<u>Dedications</u>

SDL I cannot thank you enough!
FMCALSDL
Annie & Frank G. Ahearn – Thanks for Life!
KD - My Man FSCALP
DC – DD – JA aka Buck Benz – Much Love
Mr. Reggae Music
Let's never forget Barney
Daytop Village – Millbrook – 1980
Charlie Lapera (BFAM)
Kurt Duesterdick (BFAM)

TABLE OF CONTENTS

Note

If you're a Bible beater or a moralist reading this, spare me the preaching about being dishonest, because this is a war of information, your information, to be exact. Therefore, if you want to attempt to get your information off of a website, you need to lie and create a suitable pretext.

Chapter - 1
Goodbye, Disappearing, and Hello, Deceiving

After the release of my last book, How to Disappear: Erase Your Digital Footprint, Leave False Trails, and Vanish without a Trace, I reached the point where I could no longer talk about disappearing. Between TV, radio and print, I was doing about five or six interviews a week. I would tell stories of disappearing and throw out the buzz words misinformation, disinformation and reformation. Truthfully, it became an infomercial for the book and it was no longer fun to do my disappearing sermon.

One of the last TV interviews I did about disappearing was personally enlightening. Another guest was hawking his services about protecting online privacy and it was a bunch of mumbo jumbo snake oil selling—-plain bullshit, all hat and no cattle, as they say in Texas. In my head I am thinking, what the fuck am I doing here talking about disappearing for the millionth time? In reality no one can manage or control online information--except for the information they themselves post. There is no "delete" button in this new digital dystopia that has taken over and ruined some lives. That is when I realized that the only way to combat online information is through deception. I left the TV studio and said goodbye to disappearing and hello to my little friend, deceiving.

After that the Forum section of the New York Times asked me, "In our electronic era, is it still possible to disappear into the night, as D.B. Cooper did 40 years ago?" My take has always been, "Disappearing is a double-edged sword and depends on who is searching and who is hiding." The most important thing to think about is what one does prior to disappearing and what one does with the information they cannot disappear. I answered my own question by thinking, "Why disappear when you can deceive? Therefore, make deception your tool and disappearing the byproduct."

Why Disappear, When You Can Deceive?
New York Times Forum June 2011
By
Frank M. Ahearn

The world we now live in has been invaded by an unstoppable intruder called technology. The question of whether we can disappear in this type of world is not something easily answered because the use of technology is a double-edged sword. Just as in the real world, the one who duels the best wins the war.

There are two sets of footprints: the tangible ones offline and the digital footprints that leave traces everywhere. In the online world, no "delete" buttons exist. The enemy we fight is online aggregators that disseminate information without discretion. The harsh truth is that our lives can become a digital dystopia filled with sex, lies and YouTube.

However, we can live under the radar by reducing our offline footprints. And technology can be our ally in this because it offers us tools like e-commerce, virtual mail drops, prepaid credit cards and cellphones. Additionally, we can shield our identities behind corporations, both offshore and domestic: check out Wyoming-- it's the new Belize!

In a court of law, my answer would be: "No, your honor, one cannot disappear in this electronic era." However, to a client in fear for his life, my answer would be: "Who needs to disappear when we can deceive?"

Eventually my brain is filling up on deceiving ideas and I'm figuring my next employment in life that will be beyond being Dr. Disappear and Mr. Skip-Trace. Oh, wait-- I'm an author. Why don't I write a book about deception? Hmm, okay, sounds like a plan. I pitch out the book, titled Digital Dystopia, to my publisher, with the tagline "It's Machiavelli and Sun Tzu for the digital age." My head explodes with this new concept and the publisher loves it. Like Machiavelli and Sun Tzu, I too will be remembered for the next five thousand years--as a preeminent digital deceiver of the 21st century. Talk about an ego, well, that's me.

I hook up with a cool co-writer, Hambone Jones, and we knock around the pitch and shoot it off to the publisher. The publisher comes back with a significant offer but wants the book to be larger than How to Disappear, which is about sixty thousand words. The Disappear book is what it is and provides all the tools needed in the word count. The publisher tells me the Disappear book was a little lite on words, totally discounting the fact that it was in the top ten of their Amazon's most purchased books for well over a year. This new book he wants to be 125k words. This was to be the Frank M. Ahearn How to Deceive manifesto. Now it is all about being a digital hit man.

Hambone and I sit at our laptops and we crank out the first part of the book, which is about 60k words. While this is happening we are waiting for the first part of our advance-- all in good faith.

The agent contacts me and tells me the publisher does not like the book. Hambone is quite busy and decides to remove himself from the project since the publisher is such a dick. I review the manuscript and it does need work, considering it's a first draft. What to do now? The publisher wants to bring on another writer and I'm open to the idea, and so we have some meetings.

When I wrote How to Disappear, I was putting words and experiences on paper, never once thinking about word count. My only thought and goal was to teach people how to disappear. Well, two years later it's doing well and in a number of different countries. I guess this time around the publisher expects more out of me, like a 125,000-word deception manifesto.

Looking back, I was writing a word count, not any-thing of real value. I truly believe in the use of deception to combat information, but I don't think I need to turn that deception on you by making you buy a thick book at a higher price filled with unnecessary information. Therefore, I canceled the book with the publisher and decided to write the book I believe a person needs to read in order to combat their online information. With that said, this book is all about the information--no bells, no whistles, no deception played on you. Let's rock!

Chapter 2
Privacy 2.0

For those of you who did not read How to Disappear, this article I co-wrote with Kyle Dowling (www.kdowling.com) for Playboy Magazine will get you up to speed.

Take a Crash Course in Disappearing

In our increasingly digitized world, here's the most important thing you need to know: Although privacy intrusion is often thought to take place behind the scenes, it is actually the information you voluntarily offer — -whether to Facebook or to your cable company- — that leads to loss of privacy. I know because I've spent most of my life working as a skip tracer, tracking down people who don't want to be found, for lawyers, tabloids and even the highest bidder. On the flip side, I've also helped people vanish into thin air.

I pick apart the little things in a person's life to gradually make my way into the larger things: Social Security number, credit cards and more. Personal in-formation is a dangerous tool, and it has never been more readily available. However, you can easily dissuade most pursuers with a few preventative techniques. Even if your goal isn't to disappear, you should take precautions by erasing or altering the data that third parties have on you before someone decides to use it against you.

There is a group of people I call the unknowing. I have extracted their information. For instance, a job seeker posts his opinion on a religious message board and in turn loses a prospective job at a pharmaceutical company.

All it takes is an online search and the company finds that his idealistic opinions are unsuitable for their corporate environment. Or a woman illegally collecting disability payments posts a message on a Madonna fan site. She receives a letter explaining that she has won a contest to take part in a video for her idol. She shows up and dances for the camera — -only to be arrested a week later for disability fraud. These are the unknowing. The stories are endless — -and so are the opportunities to use your information against you.

The fight to regain your privacy involves three strategies: misinformation, dis-information and reformation. Depending on your goal- — whether it's to evade a meddling ex-wife or to skip town and start over — you may not need to use all the methods. But knowing what you have at your disposal is a powerful asset.

Misinformation entails locating all the data known about you and deleting it. Run your name on various search engines. It's important to search for sites that may have your name misspelled, so trick it out with a typo or two. Also try running it with your city, phone number or zip code attached. When you find your information, contact the relevant businesses and ask them to remove the content. If they ask why, a little white lie never hurts. Be sure to tackle social net-working sites that list your family, friends, alumni and employment. These are huge danger zones.

Take a look at the services to which you subscribe. Cable companies retrieve your account by phone number, as do utility companies. Some systems will read off your street address. Ever order a pizza and see your phone number, name and address on the box label? Call the business and get that information erased. When asked for my contact info, I like to use the number made famous by Tommy Tutone: 867-5309.

Disinformation is about confusing your pursuers. To throw someone off your path, you can deliberately implant false information about yourself and create a misleading trail.

This is my favorite part of helping people disappear, and it's where I get the most creative. On your phone, cable and utility bills, do a little variation on your name. Tell the customer service representative your name is Dan instead of Don. Also, don't forget to forward your final bills to faraway places after you disconnect.

If you're looking to go deep off the radar, create a new, imaginary life for yourself. Tweet that you are moving to Chicago, use Photoshop to create images of yourself at Wrigley Field, then start a blog documenting your bogus move to Chi-Town. Anyone hunting you will focus their attention on the Windy City while you sip mai tais on the Baja peninsula. Get a debit card from a bank, put a few bucks in the account and send it to a buddy in another city. Have him use the card at supermarkets and local watering holes. If your account is compromised, a pursuer will see charges in a city you are nowhere near.

The final act of privacy is reformation, which is getting from point A to point B without being traced. The goal is to become a virtual individual, with no connection to anything physical. Prepaid phones, which can be obtained at any electronics store, are excellent tools in the disappearing trade. Register yours un-der the name Wile E. Coyote with any area code you want. For added security, never dial direct. Use a prepaid calling card.

If you need to send e-mail, wander the streets and pick up internet service for free. Communicate with a trusted recipient by using a shared e-mail account you both have the password for. Write your "e-mails" to each other by using the drafts format. Do not hit send; just save your correspondence. The recipient then reads your message and answers in the same draft document.

For expenditures, rely on prepaid cards that can be purchased over the counter with no name attached and loaded with funds via the cashier. You can also purchase a prepaid credit card by mail and load it with cash at various retail locations. (Warning: Sometimes they ask for an identifier such as your Social Security number.)

The methods I suggest here are in no way comprehensive. The more creative you are, the better. We live in a society where technology is being developed quicker than we can imagine, and our information is a precious resource for others. Timothy Leary once told us to "turn on, tune in, drop out." Today it seems that it's all about friending, tweeting, texting and blogging: anything to be a part of that third society that asks us to supply our digital DNA. A little forethought goes a long way.

Make sure you pick up a copy of *How to Disappear*.

CHAPTER 3
The Run Down

There are a few ways to get your information off of a website, such as politely asking them to remove the information, hacking the site and creating massive destruction, or creating a pretext that prompts them to remove the information. Unfortunately, asking does not always work and sometimes the request you make could backfire in your face and create the Streisand Effect.

The Streisand effect is primarily an online phenomenon in which an attempt to hide or remove a piece of information has the unintended consequence of publicizing the information more widely. It is named after American entertainer Barbra Streisand, whose attempt in 2003 to suppress photographs of her residence inadvertently generated further publicity.

As far as hacking goes, most of us do not know how to hack, so that's probably a dead end street. It is also illegal, and what's the point of that? Why get your-self jammed up?

If hacking or asking to remove your information is not a viable option, you can always attempt a pretext. Pretext is all about lying and convincing the bastard who is posting your information to remove the information.

Pretext
Creating a lie to cloak your true intentions in order to obtain or manipulate information

There is good pretext and then there is bad pretext. Good pretext is "Hi. I'm being stalked. Can you please take information down off your site?" And bad pretext is "Hi. This is the FBI. We need you to remove information from your site. That is a no-no! Never impersonate a licensed professional.

Part of my writing dilemma was trying to figure out how to take this deception in my head and put it on paper and have it make sense because some things in my head just do not make sense when I put them on paper. Then again, at times it seems a lot of things in my head make no sense. After the disappearing washed from my veins and the new blood of deception arrived, I had to figure out and somehow categorize the deception, and this is what I came up with.

The Tools of Online Deception

Digital DNA: Locating all of your online information and preparing for combat

Corp-Distort-Delete: Distorting your online accounts

The Pretext Solution: Pretexting website to remove your online information

Digital Distortion: Creating same name websites with different extensions and then stripping negative information and replacing it with positive or neutral information on your sites

Fake Digital Identities: Creating websites, blogs and social sites that all share your name

Photo Distortion and Photo Doubles: The utilization of fake photos

Propagation: Marketing the shit out of your online information

Total War: When all else fails, Total War means going head to head with the websites

These are the tools I came up with and that I believe will assist you in combating your online information. So sit back, strap in and let's go for a ride.

Chapter 4
The Short Frank M. Ahearn Bio

When people ask how I got into this crazy business, my one-liner is: I am unemployable elsewhere. To a degree, this is quite true. When people ask me why I am so good at pretext or lying, I joke about being a devious kind of guy, which I am, and ironically, it stems from a childhood event in a Chinese restaurant. For those of you who do not know my background, I offer this condensed version of the life of Frank M. Ahearn.

I grew up in New York City in a neighborhood called Inwood, made somewhat famous by Jim Carroll's Basket Ball Diaries and probably the bar capital of the world in the 1970's: it had a gin joint on almost every corner. The story goes as follows-- my parents took me and my sisters out for Chinese food because it was the communion or confirmation of one of my sisters. My father had lobster and asked the waiter if he could keep the lobster fork as a souvenir. He claimed we were tourists visiting the Big Apple, but we lived like three blocks away. The waiter said, "No problem. Keep the fork," and at that moment I learned if one lies, one can obtain things. It seemed only natural to follow in my father's footsteps.

We fast-forward to my life as a teenager. I become a drug addict, steal for drugs, get arrested and go to a drug program to avoid a life of drug abuse, crime and death. I successfully complete Daytop, the drug program which totally saved my life, and I obtain my high school GED, and now I am ready to face the world and become a man.

I get a job in a shoe store in Times Square. It's a lot of fun, but it's no future. From there I become an undercover agent in a retail store, busting dishonest employees. After a while that sucks because there is no future in undercover work. I work in the investigative office running other undercover agents, but that sucks too because I am overworked and underpaid. Eventually I become a skip tracer which is a person who locates people. I get fired and am ultimately evicted from my apartment and make my way back to my parents' apartment. I drive a taxi for a day and am offered a job as a doorman but say no.

Enlightenment sinks in and I realize that working for other people sucks. I decide to start my own skip tracing company. I make shit loads of dough. I get married and move in with my wife with all of my belongings packed in a garbage bag. I hire employees and make shit loads more money. I get audited by the IRS; I get divorced and move out with all of my belongings in one garbage bag. I file for bankruptcy and get audited by the IRS again. Finally, I become a disappear expert and build a new business. I get tired of talking about disappearing and now conjure up deception with the book you are now reading. And that, my friend, is my short bio of lying for a living. So the bottom line is, I am the best motherfucking liar in the world, so if you want to learn how to deceive, you have bought the right book.

Deception

Beguilement, deceit, bluff, mystification, bad faith, and subterfuge are acts to propagate beliefs that are not true, or not the whole truth (as in half-truths or omission). Deception can involve dissimulation, propaganda, and sleight of hand. It can employ distraction, camouflage or concealment.

Chapter 5
Pretext or Deceive

How you go about combating your online information is extremely important. Pre-text may or may not be an option. It really depends on your confidence skills and your ability to come up with a workable pretext. When I say "pretext," I do not narrow it to picking up the phone and gagging someone. Pretext can include an email claiming a photo of you is copyright-protected and insisting the website take the photo down.

In the skip tracing world we have what is called a one-shot deal, where you have only one opportunity to pretext. If you fail, you are shit out of luck and the pretext may just backfire. Remember Barbara Streisand? The one-shot deal business partner is Mr. Kick-back, one of those things you never want to happen. It's when everything blows up in your face because the person or entity you did the pretext on just doesn't believe you.

ONE SHOT DEAL
ONLY ONE CHANCE TO OBTAIN THE INFORMATION

KICK-BACK
WHEN THE PRETEXT BLOWS UP IN YOUR FACE

It is very important that you carefully consider the down-side to pretexting a website or simply requesting they take down your information. You do not want it to backfire, with the person behind the curtain deciding to call your bluff and the next thing you know, your pretext is the next big story on Gawker. If the pretext route does not work for you, then you move forward and work the tools of deception.

When one utilizes deception as a weapon to battle online information, one needs to do so with the mindset of total war. Think of the websites as belligerents who post your information or your child's information for the sheer purpose of making advertising money. What site doesn't have Google ads or click-thru links? Your information is their inventory.

The idea of total war is to use all available resources to win the battle. My purpose is to teach you the Weapons for Waging War and Winning against the Digital Enemy.

The first step in combating your online information is locating all of your Digital DNA. The best way to categorize your Digital DNA is into five digital genes of information.

The Five Genes of Digital DNA

SELF is the information that you provided to third-party sites like Facebook, LinkedIn, blogs, Twitter, online comments and any other sites where you physically participated in broadcasting.

PIV stands for Personal Information Violation, which is when someone posts your information or photo online without your permission.

DATABASE is the information that sells for $9.99 and typically consists of public records and other free online information.

COPYRIGHT INFORMATION is the information that is

protected, such as newspaper articles, photos and other content deemed as protected.

IMAGES are photos of you floating around in digital dystopia.

The next few chapters show you how you will play digital detective and hunt for everything that is known about you. The problem with information online is that it's like an ocean where the tides and currents choose their time and direction. Therefore, once you locate your information, I suggest that you wait a few days and redo the search for information you possibly missed or that was recently posted.

<u>**DIGITAL DNA**</u>
SELF
PIV
DATABASE
COPYRIGHT
IMAGES

When you join social sites and you post you contribute to your digital DNA!

Chapter 6
Digital Genes - The Self Search

The Self Search is making inventory of all of the sites you are a current member of, including old sites you participated in as well. Think about sites you may have signed up for but never participated in; there might be a few of those hanging around. When I was doing digital skip traces and background searches, I often stumbled across a duplicate LinkedIn and old blogs that had personal rants. You'd be surprised by the different sites I would discover, like the one with the married man with three kids and then the duplicate social site claiming the same man was single and ready to mingle. That old account just might leave behind that one nugget that blows it all. After you've located the third-party sites you are aware of, you need to search for the ones you do not remember.

Your search terms should be something like this: Frank M. Ahearn–disappear, Frank Ahearn – disappear, Ahearn— disappear. What you want to do is tweak your name from Frank to Francis, Ahearn Frank. People tend to misspell my name so I would include Frank Ahern by dropping the second A. It also does not hurt to translate your search into different languages--you never know what you can pick up.

Mix and match your name. Also, misspell your name, because mistakes happen. Search your full name, reverse it, and put your city next to your name and even your email address. The goal is to be as creative as possible. For those of you who are dealing with negative information, toss in the fucks, bastards, bitches and whores next to your name.

There are some simple tricks to utilize when you begin searching out your information. Think about the things you are associated and connected with--make a list. My online associations are words like disappear, privacy, skip trace, Monica Lewinsky, Alcatraz, How to and a bunch of others.

THINK CONNECTIONS
First Name – Middle Name – Last name – Titles
Birth City
Current City
Profession
Business Name
Spouse Name
Deleted Email Address
Current Email or Domain Name
Drunk Driving
Arrested
Convicted
Accused
Dismissed
High School Alumni
College Alumni
Bowling Team
VFW
S & M Club Membership

You want to keep good track of the sites you've located and it's important NOT to do anything with the sites. In the chapter **CORP-DISTORT-DELETE** we will deal with this online garbage you find. The reason I say "garbage" is because all these sites do is collect, collect and collect your information and use it to make money. They promise you the world, claiming your information is safe, but that's bullshit. We have seen hackers infiltrate the most protected of sites. Take a little time and do some research on these names.

- **Adrian Lamo**

- **Albert Gonzalez**
- **Dennis Moran**
- **Ehud Tenenbaum**
- **George Hotz**
- **HD Moore**
- **Jonathan James**
- **Kevin Mitnick**
- **Kevin Poulsen**
- **Kristina Svechinskaya**
- **Leonard Rose**
- **Rafael Núñez**
- **Robert Tappan Morris**
- **Tim Berners-Lee**
- **Weev**

I know zip shit about hacking, but I know a shitload about lying to obtain information. If I was hired to hunt down and extract information about you, the first place I would go is Facebook. It wouldn't take long for me to call in and find my way around and figure out how they operate. Facebook and other online companies protect themselves from hackers and other types of online intruders but I can't imagine it being too difficult to phone-pretext.

PRETEXT AND SOCIAL ENGINEERING ARE THE PRECURSORS TO HACKING

It's easy to figure that Facebook and other sites typically access your account by email address, just as utility and cell phone companies access your account by social security number. I would call the website corporate office or their offsite office that houses customer service or tech support and use one of several pretexts to grab the information.

"Hi, this is Frank Tromper from Steal Your Information

Company. Our systems are down. Can you bring up an email address for an account?"

This may not work the first time around because maybe their systems do not go down or maybe the department I hit up cannot bring up accounts via email addresses.

"Oh you can't bring up by email address? Can you tell me who can, or can you bring up by name?"

Remember, it's just chipping away at the stone. Every no leads to a yes.

While I am mentioning email addresses, running your email in search engines is important as well. You might locate a blog or message board you commented on or a bid on EBay. Trick out your email address the same way you did with your name.

<u>Email</u>
"info@frankahearn.com"
"@frankahearn.com"
"Frank@frankahearn.com"
"FrankAhearn@xxxxx"

Think back to those old email addresses you had in the past and tweak them too. The results of your searching will bring up different categories of information, so make sure you break down the email by mixing it around.

Chapter 7
Digital Genes - PIV Search

PIV stands for Personal Information Violation, which means someone is posting information about you online without asking your permission. PIV breaks down to known and unknown violators, the known being family and friends and the unknown everyone else making money off your information.

I find it odd that the people we know personally post our information without asking permission. Why do people assume we want our information up online or even want to be associated with the person's posting or photograph? Think about it. You're a cop, prosecutor or millionaire. Any schmuck who is able to type can locate your information because your cousin Dale in Miami posted and tagged your pictures on his Facebook page.

A year ago I saw a photo of myself on Facebook tagged with my name. Considering what I do for a living, I was shocked that this person had posted and tagged my photo. I politely requested that they remove the photo and they did.

FACIAL RECOGNITION SOFTWARE WILL SOON BE AVAILABLE TO ALL!

The first task is to begin searching social network connections. The one problem with certain sites like Facebook is that if you or a friend shared certain information or photos of you, it will not be deleted. Try to see if your friend can retag the photo.

Your search terms should include the same tweaking of your name that you did with third party sites.

REPEAT AFTER ME
SOON FACIAL RECOGNITION WILL BE AVAILABLE TO ALL!

In the future facial recognition will be able to search old newspaper photos and identify the faces in public photos.

Okay, you are going to run your name on search engines, specifically adding a social site to your name. This is somewhat tedious, but it is best to be thorough rather than cheat when hunting for your information. Also reverse the search, entering, for example, FACEBOOK, FRANK M. AHEARN.

SOCIAL CONNECTIONS
Frank M. Ahearn, Facebook
Frank M. Ahearn, LinkedIn
Frank M. Ahearn, MySpace
Frank M. Ahearn, Blogs
Frank M. Ahearn, Flickr
Frank M. Ahearn, Spouse Name
Frank M. Ahearn, Bowling Club
Frank M. Ahearn, Ostrich Farming
Frank M. Ahearn, Alumni
Frank M. Ahearn, Wife name
Children's Name, Frank M. Ahearn
Frank M. Ahearn, Friends' Names

It is important to combine your name with others because you could locate a site that is on page 97 of Yahoo and again, it could be that nugget of information that could blow your privacy boat out of the water. The thought process here is "think connected third parties."

Once you feel confident that you have located all of your information, contact your friends, family and other folks you know and ask them to re-move your information. And for your own personal social sites, do not do anything until you read the Corp-Distort-Delete chapter. With the unfriendly sites you've located, you need to make that decision--to pretext or not to pretext.

If you are going to pretext blogs or websites, think of an extreme pretext. You could claim that your sixteen-year-old daughter is being stalked by a killer soon to be released from prison. Or claim your husband is a mad lunatic out for vengeance and you need the information removed so he does not locate you. When I was pretexting, the ruse I created was a problem that I put in the lap of the person I was pretexting. Usually that person would come up with a resolution to my problem and assist me in my need.

God may help those who help themselves, but pretext helps those who need to deceive!

The sites where you do not feel comfortable pretexting will be combated through Digital Distortion and Fake Digital Identities.

Chapter 8
Digital Genes – Database Search

Database records are the big killer in the information world. Database information is the public information that is gathered by companies that then resell the information about you online to any schmuck with $9.99 and other resellers who want to pimp out your information. One such company, or should I say the master of all collectors, is Intelius. I am not going to waste any time telling you about Intelius, but I will tell you that they probably know more about your public records than you do. Pop your name, address and phone number in a search engine and you will find a link to several database sites.

The Database Search is where you will locate more offline information. It is important to run these searches so you have the intelligence to know what is available about you.

TYPES OF DATABASE INFORMATION
Name or Names
Addresses, Current & Historical
Phone Numbers, Current & Historical
Cellular Numbers, Current & Historical
Date of Birth
Motor Vehicle Searches
Real Property
Driving Records
Judgments
Tax Liens
Real and Personal Properties
Criminal Records
Social Security Death Records

Marriage Records
Divorce Records
Aircraft Registration

The best way to battle the database collectors is not to provide correct information to your offline service providers like utilities, cable, credit cards, video stores or any other places that request information. If a cable company asks for your home or work number, lie. If your credit card company wants updated information, I say, fuck those bastards and lie.

LIE – LIE – LIE - LIE

I do not want to get too deep into offline or database information because you can learn about that in How to Disappear, but the goal is to search out contact numbers and identifiers that companies-—cable, utility, water, cellular and land line-—have on you. They usually have your Social Security number, sometimes your date of birth, and sometimes your employment and contact numbers. My suggestion is to delete it all, if possible, and if not, deviate the information by giving them a different middle name or adding Jr.

Unfortunately, you cannot delete the database information. It seems that this wonderful government allows us no control but gives big business one hundred percent control over database information. One more time--if a customer service rep asks you a question, remember that the answer will be used against you!

Digital Genes – Copyright Information
Copyright news sources are the next in your digital search. One of the problems affecting those of us who may have skeletons lurking in the closet is that every newspaper and magazine from Iowa to Fiji is now uploading every issue they

ever printed. Something once visible to only a corn farmer in Iowa is now available for the world to see.

You may have made a stopover ten years ago in Iowa, gotten drunk, stripped and ridden a goat through the main street singing "The Star-Spangled Banner." The police showed up, locked you up, and you are on the local police blotter. Lucky for you that you call Chicago home and no one you know reads the Iowa Dispatch. Unfortunately for you, the Dispatch is now uploading the police blotter with your story for the whole world to see--including your wife and kids.

Copyright material is the type of information that is now on the haunt. It's that flowing river crashing through your personal levee and not stopping. The wrong newspaper hits, and you could have your very own Katrina where the government does not help, and now your shit is so fucked up you have no idea how to fix it.

Think about it. Children can now learn about their parents' hidden past. Neighbors can discover neighbors' misdeeds, boyfriends can find girlfriends' transgressions, and employees will learn about their boss's cross-dressing from a photo found online. The world will simply know about the world. Well, I say fuck that, man. Once you search out your copyrighted past, you need to move quickly. You can create some digital distortion and build a shitload of fake digital identities to take credit for the old you.

SEARCH
www.lexisnexis.com & www.newspaperarchive.com

I wish there was a magic button I could offer you to get your information out of newspapers, but there is none. I have been successful pretexting newspapers in the past and have had them take down articles that were embarrassing to clients. It was no easy task. The larger the newspaper, the easier it is, since there are more employees and everyone doesn't know everyone, unlike those working at the Duluth Dispatch. If you are attempting to pretext a newspaper, this is my suggestion.

THE PRETEXT (lying)

There are two departments you need to locate in the newspaper. The first is the Legal Department; learn who is in charge and where they are located. The second is the department that handles the online content, sometimes known as Online Platform. Once you have that information, call the main number of the newspaper and ask for Classified. Once you've reached Classified, tell them you got the wrong department and you need Online Platform. The reason for the multiple transfers is that it will hide your number on their caller ID.

Once you've reached the Online Platform department, explain that you are calling from the Legal Department, Mr. So-and-So's office, and explain that an article is posted online and may need to come down because of pending litigation. If the article needs to be removed, how would you go about requesting this? Once you know, do your thing.

WHEN YOU PRETEXT, YOU ALWAYS USES A PREPAID CELL PHONE

Chapter 9
Digital Genes – Image Search

The final search for your **Digital DNA** is an Image Search. This is a simple search so there's no need for me to bloat the chapter. You are going to use the same methods you used with your name. There were times when I was unable to locate information on a subject, and sure enough, when I put the subject's name in a search engine and clicked images, a photo came up. The photo led me to some obscure website that assisted me in getting closer to the subject. When searching for images, use your associated words, as I explained in the previous chapter. Twist and turn your information.

Frank M. Ahearn, Disappear
Frank M. Ahearn, Wife
Frank M. Ahearn, Ex-wife
Frank M. Ahearn, Venice Beach
Frank M. Ahearn, Digital Hit Man
Frank M. Ahearn, Paris France

All of the information you've located is your Digital DNA. If you do not do something about the information you've located, it will remain a part of your past and become a part of your future.

Chapter 10
It is Your Digital DNA

I am sure some of you are thinking, so what's the big deal about my information floating around online? The big deal is that the information is being gathered, and it will be used against you some time in the near future in civil, divorce and even criminal cases. Unfortunately, the near future could be too late for you to react to a situation.

Social Security numbers are a good example of what is to come in the future. Social Security Numbers were first used in the mid-thirties, when the government devised the New Deal's Social Security program, which focused on the three R's: Relief, Recovery and Reform. And in less than three months, over 25 million Social Security numbers were assigned. The original purpose of the number was to be able to track an individual's accounts in the Social Security program.

Today you need a Social Security number to exist in society. If you want a driver's license, bank account, cable TV, utilities, a mortgage, an apartment, credit cards, credit check, car insurance, medical assistance at a doctor's office or hospital, or even to go to college or apply for a job, you need to provide those nine evil numbers. To a degree it is a brand on your identity like that on the side of a cow.

A funny tidbit: until the 1980s, Social Security cards expressly stated that the SS number and the card were not to be used for identification purposes. That message has since been removed.

Not getting too deep, there is a law an act called HAVA, Help America Vote Act that requires states to verify the information of newly registered voters in Federal elections. Each state must establish a computerized statewide voter registration list and verify new voter information with the state's Motor Vehicle Administration (MVA). If the voter does not have a driver's license, the state is required to verify the last four digits of the new voter registrant's Social Security number. The funny thing is, if you have the last four digits of a person's SS number, it's easy to toy with and figure out the rest of the digits. Sorry but I am not going to explain how.

My point is that when something is introduced in society, eventually someone down the road finds new uses for that information. Unfortunately, in the digital realm it's some techie who comes up with the bright idea of utilizing that information for profit, and then Big Brother uses it for control. I find that the perfect reason for wanting to rid the Internet of personal information.

Chapter 11
A Few More Places to Search

The Way Back Machine

At www.archive.org, is a digital time capsule that enables users to see archived versions of web pages across time. Search your name, blogs and websites you have been associated with for information. If you find an association there, I believe the only way to combat it is to create a pretext.

Marriage & Divorce Records

These records vary from state to state and county to county. If you are searching for your own records, search out the county and the city you took the big leap in, and see what shows. I just entered my name and my ex-wife's name like this online: "Frank M. Ahearn & Ex-wife," and an address where we lived almost thirty years ago showed up with a history of other people who owned the house.

Aircraft Registration

http://registry.faa.gov/aircraftinquiry

Political Donations

Your party preference is available online by searching your name for donations. Search out your political donations at www.opensecrets.org.

A woman contacted me a while back and asked if I could assist her in dealing with her online information. She was going to do some traveling in countries where abductions of the wealthy can happen. When I ran her name online, there was one posting that showed that her father had sold his company for millions of dollars.

This part would have been easy to distort by creating digital identities, but there was the larger issue of her political donations. Her donations were top dollar, and numerous. It was easy to recognize that she had a lot of money.

Copyright Records
When I search my name, it comes up with publishers' names and addresses [for contact?]. You may have copyrighted something and used your home or business address. Consider using a mail drop: www.copyright.gov.

The Journalist Tool Box
The Tool Box is an amazing source for online records: www.journaliststoolbox.org.

NNDB
The site www.nndb.com is an intelligence aggregator that tracks the activities of people who are considered noteworthy, both living and dead. But it exists mostly to document the connections between people, many of which are not always obvious. A person's otherwise inexplicable behavior is often understood by examining the crowd that person has been associating with.

The National Archives
The site www.archives.gov is The National Personnel Records Center (NPRC), one of the National Archives and Records Administration's (NARA) largest operations. The NPRC is the central repository of personnel-related records for both the military and civil services of the United States Government.

CensusFinder
The mission of www.censusfinder.com is to provide access to

all available census records online. This includes both free and paid subscriptions.

Ancestry

The site www.Ancestry.com helps you search for historical records about your family and start your free family tree.

Ellis Island & the Statue of Liberty

The site www.ellisisland.org is simply amazing. That is where you can search names of immigrants and find out what ships they came on to America great tools for searching your genealogy.

New databases are always popping up, so do some looking around. I am sure some geek somewhere has created a new one using your information.

Chapter 12
Putting the Pieces Together

During the writing of this book, a woman by the name of Lake contacted me and asked for some skip tracing advice. I am usually reluctant to offer any, but I did a few basic searches on her and was able to confirm who she was; she did not score high on the Frank M. Ahearn litmus test of potential clients. Check out her email, below. Also, I was bored and could not think of what chapter to work on, and the good fortune of her misfortune turned into our fortune.

The email is a little confusing but the scenarios was too so it might take a second or third reading exactly understand. It is a good example how a person can search out information from their kitchen table or even need to hire a professional.

I don't even know where to begin with this. I am not really looking to disappear, although that wouldn't be the worst thing. I feel like a complete and utter moron, but I was deceived by someone via the Internet. This went on for about ten years! They live in New Jersey and I live in California. We've never met in person (I know, big red flag. Hindsight and all that.) It was never about money, as this person, who played the parts of a multitude of family members and kept it all straight, seemed most interested in our friendship and claimed to have an abundance of money. They sent me all sorts of stuff over the years. Far more than I ever sent them. The stories were SO detailed. When I think about it, which I do often right now, my mind is just blown. I celebrated births and mourned deaths with this person. We baked together and watched the same movies, talked at length about our friends and families, spoke on the phone almost daily, traded recipes and photographs. Hundreds of photographs.

The photographs are the most disturbing part, though, and are the only reason I am not completely washing my hands of the whole thing and moving on. I've done some research and it seems the photographs are of unsuspecting family members or very close friends and their young child. I was also sent inappropriate pictures of what--I was to believe — were my friends. I don't believe these other people know anything about this and I suspect my so-called friend is using or will use the photos to deceive someone else. In some of the photos a woman is wearing a shirt we sent or is holding a bag of coffee we roasted and sent. I suspect that my alleged friend had told her friends/family members she has a friend who sends things and has shared them with these friends/family members and then photographed things as proof to me that she is who she says she is.

I would like to figure out who these people in the photo are so that I can tell them what I know, and then I want to put it behind me and get on with my life. I just worry that my so called friend has already laid the groundwork with the people so they may be expecting a call from a "crazy person" she met on the Internet. I don't know how best to contact them and have them at least hear me out so that I know they have been made aware.

I have most of a phone number I was able to get off of a dog tag in a photo, and I do know what area they live in. I was able to get the real woman's first name and the first name of their child. I can't figure out the man's name but I am poring over the photographs and am looking at them through different eyes, looking for any clues at all. I was able to see the deceitful woman's reflection in sunglasses in a few of the photographs of the man, and she is definitely NOT the person she claimed was taking the photos she sent me. I was also able to find her real daughter's blog, which has several photos of the real woman as well as photos of the unsuspecting woman and her daughter, so I know they are related or close friends.

I'd like to meet with these people face to face so that I can KNOW for sure I am speaking to them, but I don't know how to do that without *calling them first and potentially freaking them out. My family and friends have known about my friendship for the entire time and are stunned by all of this, so I can't even imagine how an unsuspecting person would take this. I am just an idiot for trusting, so I deserve what I get, but the people in the photos are being completely exploited and are completely unaware. They don't deserve this. Any advice would be so greatly appreciated.*

This email took me on a new journey as well as dropping me back in the trenches for a little skip tracing action. At first the email confused me a bit, so I asked Lake to clarify some of the information. The gist is that Lake met New Jersey in a chat room for those involved in poly-amorous relationships.

Lake, who lived in California, met her new friend in 2000. The friend claimed she lived in New Jersey along with her husband, her boyfriend and her children. I know--strange. Over the ten-year period, Lake and the New Jersey triangle grew close in friendship. It was a relationship of sharing birthdays, holidays and the typical ups and downs of life through phone calls, emails and Christmas cards. The two triangular families never had the opportunity to meet. Something always came up, but Lake thought nothing of it. Throughout the years, birthday and Christmas gifts were exchanged, and hundreds of photos were sent via email. Those photos included vacations at the shore, teen graduations and everything else Middle America does and shares in their Hallmark moments.

The morning Lake contacted me, she was reading an article about someone who defrauded another person via a digital relationship, meaning one in which the parties involved met through a digital medium or social networking site and have never met in in real life.

Maybe I am old-fashioned, but I do not understand how people develop close relationships with those they have never physically met. I can understand the digital face being an acquaintance or someone to pass on stupid email jokes to, but a real friend? I just cannot connect.

The article left an ominous feeling in Lake. There were a lot of similarities between her relationship and the relationship of the person in the article who was defrauded by her Internet friend. The husband in the New Jersey family worked as manager of a supermarket. Lake picked up the phone and called the supermarket, but there was no Mr. New Jersey working there. Being a little slick, Lake called the district office of the supermarket chain and posed as someone from United Parcel Service with a damaged package for Mr. New Jersey. The words of the office manager hit Lake hard: he claimed there never was and never had been a Mr. New Jersey who worked for the company.

Lake was shocked. Had she and her mate been duped by this alleged couple, if so why? There was never any money loaned nor were large ticketed items sent to New Jersey. From all appearances, it seemed like a genuine friendship--well, maybe a little more than that, perhaps an intimate photos?

Lake began sifting through the ten years of photos and located one of the New Jersey couple holding their cat. She noticed the cat had an ID tag and figured she would magnify the photo and see what was on the tag. She was able to capture all but the last digit of the phone number on the cat's tag. She thought it was odd that she did not recognize the couple's usual phone number. She ran the number through a reverse listing site, inserting different last digits in numerical order, from zero to nine.

Reverse listing is a way to identify the owner of a published phone number. However being on the reverse listing site does not mean it is accurate or up-to-date.

One of the numbers was a hit and showed as a published number. The name was that of Mr. & Mrs. New Jersey, but not at the address Lake knew. Actually, it was in a different city, not too far from the PO Box where she sent cards, letters and gifts.

The man in the photo had a hat from a university alumni association, and Lake searched the university and found the Mr. New Jersey in the photo was an alumnus of the school who at present was? a doctor at a local hospital. Lake searched the hospital and found more photos of the alleged Mr. New Jersey. It was if her triangular family and friends had stolen someone else's photo identity.

After discovering the real Mr. New Jersey, it was easy for Lake to see that the ten-year relationship was a total fraud. All the vacation photos, holiday photos and even a few compromising photos were of another couple, not the friend she believed to be Mrs. New Jersey.

Lake wanted me to help her figure out who was who in this affair. I was curious about who she spoke with on the phone and learned that she and the woman spoke freely, calling each other back at will, although when Lake called Mr. New Jersey's cell phone to say hello, she got only a voice mail. His MO was to call her back. Too bad for Lake that she was unaware of Spoof Card and other software that disguises and changes voices, even female to male.

The next step for the amateur sleuth was to run Mr. New Jersey's name on Google images, where Lake found a blog that had a photo of Mr. & Mrs. New Jersey, who were identified as the blogger's neighbors. The woman in the photo was the woman she had believed to be her friend all of these years. The young man who wrote the blog had several others, and Lake stumbled onto a blog about him and his family. The blogger wrote about various trips which, coincidentally, were the same trips Mrs. New Jersey claimed she and Mr. New Jersey had taken.

The young blogger had a photo of himself and his mother. Lake wondered if this was the real person she had been in contact with over the years. The blogger son was somewhat of a social networking junky and had a Flickr account and a YouTube channel that put the crazy puzzles together.

Lake searched photo after photo for more clues. One such photo was of a car in a driveway; the house number was the same as the house number picked up from the reverse listing site and the phone number she had identified. Then came the shocker: one of the photos taken of Mr. New Jersey showed a reflection in his glasses of a woman, who was, in fact, the blogger's mother. Who was this mysterious woman in the photograph? Lake wondered how she could go about identifying her.

On Flickr the blogger had a photo of himself in his driveway. The house number was only two digits away from that of the real Mr. & Mrs. New Jersey. Lake did a reverse listing on the address and checked tax records. Mrs. Fraud was identified, and Lake located photos of her on various Websites, including her business website. She cleaned houses.

Did Mrs. Fraud steal her neighbors' photos from their computer? Was she a friend of theirs on Facebook who downloaded the photos? And there's the question of the few compromising photos--how did she obtain them?

It's unfortunate for Lake that she was duped all of these years, but more unfortunate are the real Mr. and Mrs. New Jersey. They have no clue that their neighbor is playing such a sick digital game with their identities.

Lake wanted to contact the neighbors and make them aware of what was going on. However, I suggested not doing so, considering the extreme nature of the fraud this person had played. The really scary part is that Mrs. Fraud knows practically everything about Lake and her family. Therefore, exposing the truth could put Lake and her family in serious danger. There will probably be no closure for Lake. This is something that needs to be resolved by her walking away. A ten-year alleged friendship was exposed in one afternoon, all because of a cat tag in a photo. My suggestion is, Whether you're tri-, bi-, or solo, find your friends in the world of bricks and mortar, and if not, at the very least, be cautious in digital relationships.

At the moment someone could be downloading the photos on your social site and posing as you and your family.

One of the reasons I included this chapter is to show how an average person can go about doing their own online investigation without ever leaving their computer.

Chapter 13
The Pretext Solution

Pretexting is the fine art of creating a lie in order to obtain information. I love pretexting and seriously miss the days of walking into my office and having several employees banging out work. The idea of being able to sit at my desk and convince employees of phone companies, utility companies and airlines located in different parts of the world to give me the information I wanted--well, it was a huge rush.

Most of the people who contact me typically ask how they can go about deleting their online information. Obviously, there are no delete buttons that offer such action on websites, and I do not think it will be happening any time soon. However, through pretext it is possible to delete your information from websites, but there is no single? full-swoop action across digital dystopia.

The first thing to understand about pretext is that it can be illegal in certain ways. You cannot pick up the phone and claim to be a licensed professional such as a lawyer, doctor, CPA or any type of law enforcement officer. You cannot pretext (lie) banks, insurance companies, or telephone companies, or pose as an employee or representative of such entities. I am sure there are more pretext you cannot do, but this gives you the idea. Eventually, I believe pretexting for profit and gain will be illegal. Damn the man!

During the pretext days, I was making money hand over fist. Our biggest biller was extracting information from the phone companies. I existed in an underground world of gray-area information until some dumb ass private investigators began offering phone records on their websites. One day I redesigned my website and offered phone records, and later that day I took it down, realizing how stupid it was to offer gray area information for sale.

I saw the writing on the wall and knew it was only a matter of time until Big Brother outlawed my skills. I figured it was best to put myself out of business and not wait for the FTC to roll my way. This decision wreaked financial havoc in my life. The last month we pretexted, US phone companies brought in upwards of fifty thousand dollars in billing. From then on I lost about seventy percent of my income. That truly sucked.

I thought of various solutions, like moving to the Cayman Islands and doing the work offshore. However, we were not the only ones to consider moving offshore and pretexting from there. Federal law specifically states that pretexting is a crime that crosses borders. Therefore, from the sunny beaches of Cayman Brac it still would have been a crime to extract and sell phone records. This was the absolute end for me. However, there was the incident of the helicopter above my house and the story of the fat man that sealed the deal and ended my pretexting career.(Sorry, but you need to pick up How to Disappear to read those stories.)

I fast-forward and find myself in the weird disappearing venture writing a book about how to disappear. From there I become a media whore, sharing disappearing with anyone who will listen. I got sick of the disappearing mumbo jumbo and stopped talking about it and then found myself in the world of deceiving.

When I stopped talking about disappearing and began talking about deception, a few people contacted me, asking for help.

The usual story was that a newspaper had an article about them and they wanted it to be removed. The only way that was going to happen was via pretext. To be honest, as much as I love pretext, I didn't really want to go back to that world because I felt like I'd lost my edge.

Onward! If you are going to attempt a pretext in order to rid a website of your information, you should research carefully and confirm that the place you are going to pretext is the origin of the information. I get Google alerts that notify me when a news article or blog contains my name, website or book. One news article can land on fifty blogs and websites, and so can the origin of the information. Aggregators are the big enemy of information! They spread your information all over the net.

An aggregator is a website or computer software that collects information from multiple online sources.

Types of Aggregators

News: A computer software or website that aggregates news from other news sources

Poll: A website that aggregates polling data for upcoming elections

Review: A website that aggregates reviews of movies or other products or services

Search: A software that runs on a user's computer and fetches, filters, and organizes a specific search from various search engines

Social Network: A collection of content from multiple social network services

Video: A website that collects and organizes online video sources

Once again, if you plan to pretext a company to take down your information, make sure that it is the origin or the site that is spreading the disease. If I were hired to pretext information off a site, I would create an email address like **TusconCopyRightProtectionServicesofAmercia@** and email with a demand for the site to remove the information because of copyright protection.

IMAGES

If a website has online photos of you and you want them removed, contact them and run them the line about copyright infringement. It is usually easier for a website to remove a photo than to search out its ownership. On some photos or in news articles you will see the credit for the photographer. Create an email address using his name. Oh, wait! That could be illegal.

Do remember the danger of pretexting a website or blog is that it can kick back and make matters worse. As I mentioned, the Streisand effect is an online phenomenon in which an attempt to hide or remove a piece of information has the unintended consequence of publicizing the information more widely. It is named after the American entertainer Barbra Streisand, whose attempt in 2003 to suppress photographs of her residence inadvertently generated further publicity. That from our friends at Wiki.

Thus, again, the act of pretexting could create a new story that just might become twice as popular as the article you wanted quashed. Pretext is a calculated risk and there are never any guarantees of the outcome.

I know I said this before, but a reminder never hurts anyone. Therefore, if you are going to pretext, make sure you make the call from a prepaid phone and dump the phone when you are finished. If you send out emails to blogs and websites to get rid of your online information, make sure you use a free email address that you eventually delete. I would also consider sending that email from a wireless connection you find on the street.

The solution by pretext is more of a crap shoot than an actual solution, but a chapter titled "Pretext Crapshoot" just doesn't sound all that positive. In reality, pretexting has always been a crap shoot in my life, and it's an art, not a science.

The Art of Pretext

I believe that any piece of information that exists can be accessed or manipulated in a phone conversation or written email via pretext. All you need to do is create a reason why the person at the other end should give you or change the information.

So the big question is how to go about creating a pretext that works. The real art is taking the company rep you are talking to on a journey. If the rep is a young guy, I'm going to shoot the shit about going to the Caribbean and chilling out with the fellas. If the rep is an older woman, I am going to talk about my daughter who just got married or had a baby. If it's a younger woman, it's all about me taking my kids to Disney World, and then I hit her up with my problem.

The problem is, I need extra money so I was hoping we could go over the calls on my bill so I can turn them in and get reimbursed before we go on the trip.

THE ART OF PRETEXT

1. I offer a scenario – Kids to Disneyworld
2. I offer a problem – I need extra money
3. I hope – I do not request
4. I suggest an action – I do not ask
5. I create a small sense of urgency - with a limited window of time

When I taught a new employee to pretext, the most important aspect was how they asked for the information. I would never have the skip tracer state they need to go over the phone numbers on a phone bill, or need the address of a customer, or the balance in a checking account. It was always done to the tune of "I need to go over the calls. What are you showing in account?" I always compared pretexting to dating: when you are out on the hunt to meet someone and you hook up, you don't say, "Let's go back to my place and jump in the sack." You soften the blow and suggest a drink at your place. The intention result is the same.

If I had a phone number and I needed to get the name or address, and the phone company was busting my balls, I would call the phone number directly. "This is Frank Tromper with FMA Shipping. I have water-damaged package and need the correct shipping location." Notice: I asked for the address without directly requesting it.

Pretexting larger companies is a lot easier than smaller companies. The simple reason is the number of employees. In larger companies it's all about "Every no leads to a yes." Smaller companies are usually a one-shot deal, and sometimes it is wiser to pass on one-shot deals.

The one positive about the Pretext Solution is that if you are successful in the ruse, it kills the bad information but keeps the good. Unfortunately, this is a full-time battle you need to continue to fight. Today you may have pretexted your way off of five websites, but two months from now that information could surface via an aggregator you missed or a blog that never ranked on a search engine.

IN THE WORLD OF PRETEXT EVERY NO LEADS TO A YES JUST LIKE DATING.

Chapter 14
The Porn Identity

Meet Jason Porn, who is now in his mid-thirties, married with two and a half kids, drives a minivan and lives in the suburbs. Jason is a well-respected senior vice president of an investment bank, and his wife is a substitute teacher in the fine school their children attend.

One afternoon, like many of us, Jason decided to Google himself. Unfortunately for Jason, the past he wished he had forgotten finally caught up with him. In college Jason and a few buddies produced a low-budget porn movie that was now for sale and in big black letters it read "PRODUCED BY JASON PORN." The serious kicker was that the advertising showed a photo of him and his buddies. Jason did not know that one of his buddies had sold the right to the film fifteen years prior.

A big "uh-oh" shivers and crashes in Jason's head as he imagines his life falling to pieces with everyone discovering his secret. Who you gonna call? Not Ghost Busters or some bullshit company that charges $9.99 to manage and remove online information, but the Digital Hit Man, Frank M. Ahearn.

Taking a look at the porn site and other information found about Jason Porn, I didn't really see it as a big deal. The porn film was no "Deep Throat." It was a cheap retro that took up space and sold for $4.99. My first suggestion to Jason was to work on getting his photo offline. My first step was to set up a bogus photography website like JasonPornPhotos that had a bunch of photos loaded, including the one of him on the porn box.

I contacted the porn website politely, requesting that they remove the photo since there was a copyright infringement, and I further stated that the original producers of the film did not have the rights to the photo, either. Many legitimate websites post photos and do not have permission or own the rights to a photo. So it's worth the bluff to contact them and request the removal.

Dear Webmaster,

My name is Jason Porn and I would like to know who I can contact to request that a photo be removed from your website due to copyright infringement.

Thank you.
Jason Porn

This was a polite act of deception. The webmaster returned an email asking which photo, and in return I identified the photo in question. In a few days the photo was removed from the porn site.

Moral of the story: sometimes you get more by lying than by honesty. The immoral moral of the story is, It's sometimes better to deceive.

If you do not have the means to build a website to put a bunch of photos on to appear as if you are photographer, no problem. Use the free MySpace or Flickr, or create an email address that has the word "copyright" or "infringement" in the name, like infringement@frankahearn.com, and let the website you are contacting see that you are serious, and hopefully, as in Jason's case, they will find it easier to remove than to spin their wheels asking for proof of copyright.

Getting his photo removed was a score, but taking it a step further to ask them to remove his name from the associated content could cause some blowback.

Blowback is the espionage term for unintended consequences of a covert operation that are suffered by the civil population of the aggressor government.

The removal of the photo also removed a huge burden from Jason Porn's shoulders. But it was important to remind him that he still needed to search for that photo every so often, so it would not pop up somewhere else in the future.

Karl Von Clausewitz wins the Frank M. Ahearn Kick Ass Award and was on the money when he stated, "Pursue one great decisive aim with force and determination." Now the goal was to separate Jason's name from the porn website.

Karl Philipp Gottfried von Clausewitz was a Prussian soldier and German military theorist who stressed the moral and political aspects of war.

FAKE DIGITAL IDENTITIES
This is a simple example of Fake Digital Identities, which I discuss in detail later in the book. I develop about 25 websites that incorporate the name of my client like Frank Tromper or Jason Porn and use many extensions like com, net, org, info, ca, de and others. What I did was create a variety of websites, some with content pertaining to horns, shoes, books, Buenos Aires, chickens and lot of other fun stuff. On top of that, I opened a Google AdSense account and put ads on the sites. I also opened an Amazon Associate account and offered books and products for sale.

Opening the Google and Amazon accounts got the websites onto search engines. Then I created one site that was all about porn, and I included the information about Jason's Porn from the past. However, that site has a photo of some fake person who takes credit for the dirty deeds of my client.

Now when Jason searches his name online, there is a shitload of pages that incorporate his name. You will find the beet company in Indiana, the sleeveless shirt company in Toronto, the nonexistent bookstore in Cleveland and a bunch of other businesses, although the most important site is that of the doctor of porn himself, who lives in Cicely, Alaska, and spends much of his time hanging at the Brick Bar talking with his friend Fleischman about the good old days of producing porn films.

Very Important

If you are creating Fake Digital Identity websites, it is important, important, and super-important that you do not use any of your own identifiers. It could be rather difficult to explain to your wife or your boss why you own fifteen websites about craziness.

Consider setting up a domestic corporation or an offshore IBC (International Business Corporation) and buying the domain names via your corporation. This way they are owned by a company, not you. With the offshore company you can get a bank account and a debit card from the bank and pay for all your deception with a little privacy and have some peace of mind. Also, pay for the websites for a full year so they are parked and you do not need to deal with them.

I do not know if it is illegal to provide false information on your website's WHOIS information I say check your local, state and federal laws before doing so.

To get some domain names using country-specific extensions, you need either an address or a local presence in the country. I am not telling you to break the law, but you could provide an address of a mail drop even if you do not own a mail drop in that country.

Early on in my deceptive practices I learned the hard way. I built a bunch of websites with country-specific domain extensions and gave a bogus address. I didn't have a mail drop but I made up the address, never thinking the hosting company would verify it. A week later around twenty websites were shut down and it was a pain in the ass and a HUGE embarrassment with my client. Do your research on country-specific domain extensions.

IMPORTANT!

Some domain extensions cannot be hidden so before you buy and build do your research

Chapter 15
Corp-Distort-Delete

In my original manifesto about deception I wrote a chapter "TOS," terms of service. I basically researched a bunch of websites' and social sites' Terms of Service and, besides being super-boring, they all share one common feature--the right to use your information. The "I AGREE" button you click gives your gold away—your information. After being bored to death, I decided not to include the long-winded chapter about sites' terms of service. The truth is, you're an adult. Read the small print yourself. When you do, you will see that it not to your benefit to click on "I agree."

I AGREE SIMPLY MEANS I GIVE YOU THE RIGHT TO USE MY INFORMATION!

Technology is wonderful and mind-blowing at the same time--we can snap a photo on top of the Eiffel Tower and text it or email it to friends and family in most parts of the world. We can listen to music on tiny devices and download our favorite movie. It's all cool but I am sure this is going to be stone-age technology in less than twenty years after writing this book. For me, I dig the access to informatio but I do not like what I have to give up in order to obtain that information--a digital footprint. In time, I believe all of us will have a digital security number that traces and logs all of our online movement. Let me put that in bold print:

In time, I believe all of us will have a digital security number that traces and logs all of our online movement.

In the world of third-party sites, it has become acceptable business practice for people who indulge to give up privacy and allow business entities carte blanche with their goods. Before you cancel access to an account that you participate in read its TOS and obtain a better understanding of what it does with your information after you are excommunicated.

Every website has a different meaning for the word "delete". From the TOS of different sites I've learned that one will delete photos but another will not delete photos you shared. Also, when you hit "delete," it may take down the postings you have shared but it does not delete the actual information from the website's internal system. Another site I came across stated that it keeps the information on file for an indeterminate amount of time. What is that, 100 years?

Hitting the "agree" button allows a site to keep your information even after your relationship hits the rocks. The "I love you" postings or the stupid photos of you at a party with your ex-loved one wearing the same shirt because it's cute may never go away. Imagine the look on your new partner's face when he or she pops your name into Google and begin searching out your Digital DNA. They'll strike some sour gold, and there it is--you and the ex, all cute. Perhaps they somehow stumble onto your posting and vows of love. Perish the thought and make me puke!

When a person deletes their online account, it does not disappear into thin air. It remains in a holding-cell limbo. Just in case you are involved in a legal battle or court case, the systems needs access to your E-DISCO, which has nothing to do with "Saturday Night Fever," but it can be your worst nightmare then the white suit Travolta sported.

Electronic Discover gives law enforcement and the legal system total access to your Digital DNA. In plain English, that means if you texted a dirty thought to your secret lover, tweeted nasty things about your mother-in-law, posted derogatory remarks about your boss, emailed a nude photo, left or received an embarrassing voice mail, or did anything else that exists in our third life of technology, you run the risk of being served a subpoena.

Even worse, imagine yourself caught up in the middle of a Casey Anthony-like trial, where your dark and dirty texts and emails are televised for your friends and family to see. We all have skeletons in the technology closet, so ask yourself if you really want to participate in something that has the possibility of being seen by the world. Please do not think, **"IT'S NOT GOING TO HAPPEN TO ME."** It happens to people all the time. What makes you special?

To read more, jump to Electric Serve, **E-DISCO** and Landlocked chapter.

When you indulge in technology, think about it from a different perspective. Besides having access to your information, there are others who do, too, like hackers, law enforcement officers, lawyers, employees of the site and perhaps a suspicious mate. Therefore, with every smooch, lick and yum you email text or post, many eyes can peek into that so-called private and sometimes indiscreet world of yours.

Just a tiny bit more about Term of Service. One company I researched has you agreeing that you grant them non-exclusive, transferable, sub-licensable, royalty-free, world-wide license to use any IP content that you post on or in connection with... Imagine that you post pictures of your kids and you grant a company these rights.

WORLDWIDE LICENSE TO USE ANY IP CONTENT THAT YOU'VE POSTED!

Another site reserves the right to modify the agreement you signed at any time and from time to time, with each such modification to be effective upon posting. Therefore, the service that you signed up for, as well as the agreement you made, can be changed whenever the site so desires. Imagine that a company can modify the terms of the agreement after you've read and agreed to the terms. My ramble about TOS is done!

When I was doing skip tracing, the utility companies were the promised land of information. If a target I was hunting had utilities in 1953, there was a strong possibility that the utility company still had a record of that account. I don't mean that the records were hidden down in a dusty basement in a cardboard box; they were actually accessible on the phone from a customer service rep. Websites are following the path of utility companies and keeping it all.

I said this before--if I were hired to hunt down and extract information about you, the first place I would go is Facebook. It wouldn't take long for me to call in and find my way around and figure out how they operate. Most organizations are set up in a similar fashion. Online companies like Facebook protect themselves from hackers and other types of online intruders. Some seem to forget that pretexting and social engineering were the precursors to computer hacking. I think most companies pay no attention to skip tracers or offline information thieves. I won't even go into the simplicity of extracting information from a company that outsources. Well, on second thought, it's fucking simple to pretext outsourced customer service.

As I said before it's easy to figure that Facebook and most other sites access your account through your email address, just as utility and cell phone companies usually access your account by phone number or Social Security number. I would call in to the website's corporate office or their offsite office that houses customer service, tech support, whatever, and use one of several pretexts to grab the information.

"Hi, this is Frank Tromper from The Digital Hit Man Company. Our systems are down. Can you bring up an email address for an account?"

This may not work the first time around, because maybe their systems do not go down, or maybe the department I reach cannot bring up accounts via email addresses.

"Oh, you can't bring up by email address? Can you tell me who can bring up by email address or the customer's name?"

IT'S CHIPPING AWAY AT THE STONE, AND EVERY NO LEADS TO A YES!

I really believe there should be a law that requires companies to delete information of ALL accounts after X number of months. But why should they delete your information when someday the data could be used elsewhere? I think you now understand that when you shut down a site, blog or message board, you have zero control of the information you leave behind. However, before you shut down a website, blog or social site, it is important to create a little corporate distortion with Corp-Distort-Delete.

CORP-DISTORT-DELETE
DISTORTING INFORMATION PRIOR TO DELETING ONLINE ACCOUNTS

My thought is, why leave all of that correct information for someone to use? Distort it and paint it with some graffiti. It is like sabotaging your information with hopes of blurring the truth since you cannot actually blow it up.

EMAIL DISTORTION

The first action is to change your email address even though your original contact will never be deleted. I suggest that you change your email several times and really distort the information. Also, this is something you should do a good while prior to taking down your page.

If my log-in email is FrankAhearn@something, I would create FrankAhearnIowa@liar4hire, FrankAhern@g FrankAherne@, FrankOhern@ and so on. I would do this every few days, just changing things over a period of time. I would have the actual email address accounts and send bullshit emails to various people, places and companies.

I would email fake lovers, have conversations with aliens and confirm lunch meetings with Abe Lincoln. Perhaps talk about the money you have hidden in Oceania or the house you purchased in Oz. Make it enjoyable. This way, if the information is accessed by hacker, big brother or lawyer, you let the snoops figure out what's real and what's not. In the great words of Frank M. Ahearn: Fuck those bastards! Serve them up some bullshit.

WALL DISTORT

If you are part of a social site where you can post or share, you need to do some graffiti and tarnish the posted information. Use your imagination and post about moving, marrying a fake person, getting a job as a surgeon.

Why leave the information clean for some other person or company to make money on your information? I would post messages to as many strangers as possible and create as much bullshit wall dialogue as possible.

PHOTO DISTORT

If you've posted or shared photos, I would retag them and use different names. This may not affect photos that have already been tagged, but it could cause problems with actually identifying you. For example, if you posted and tagged several photos of yourself, load photos of people of different races and tag them with your name then start sharing and posting. I am sure your current friends will think you're nuts, but when it comes to deception, one must be bold.

TORT DISTORT

Some states are allowing process to be served electronically, meaning if a process server cannot physically locate you to serve process for a lawsuit, they can find an email address or MySpace account and legally serve process electronically. What you need to do is scrub and strip any and all identifiers from social media accounts, because, for all you know, this might be the digital trace that is accepted as a good serve.

If you happen to have accounts on social media sites out there, like LinkedIn, floating in limbo and you forgot to delete them, those accounts could be served process and you would not know about it, and if it is a civil case, you could possibly lose by default and have a judgment placed against you.

Sabotage is a deliberate action aimed at weakening another entity through sub-version, obstruction, disruption, destruction, and Frank M. Ahearn's Corp-Distort-Delete.

STEPS OF CORP-DISTORT
EMAIL DISTORTION
WALL DISTORT
PHOTO DISTORT
TORT DISTORT
DELETE
HIT DELETE AND SAY GOODBYE!

Chapter 16
Don't Shit Where You Eat

"Don't shit where you eat" is one of those crude terms I dislike hearing and saying, but it is also a wise piece of advice some should embrace. For those who utilize the digital world to lie, cheat and email, take heed and learn from fallen comrades. One click of the wrong button can take your world and spiral it down and out of control. Two words: Anthony Weiner, the guru of digital dumbasses. Here is a guy who appeared to have it all, a rising and shining career that pointed to the Mayor's seat--the Mayor of New York, not Mayberry. Our guru Anthony made a grave error--he shat where he ate.

Anthony was flirting with some babes via Twitter--what a twit. He sent off a photo to a chick and instead of hitting private, he hit public--big dumbass! Then arrive's his lame excuse that his account was hacked, but that was crap. The Weiner scandal was big news in New York. He eventually resigned and his bright future was flushed down the bowl.

I do not think I need to give you 20 examples of people who have made stupid mistakes via social sites. If you search the net, you will find plenty of stories of social adultery and those who got stung. You have two options that can assist in protecting you from such exposure. One is not to be deceptive, and the other is not to utilize social networking accounts in your deception.

If you are going to be deceptive, purchase your own domain name with a prepaid credit card and give a bogus WHOIS.

Use that domain email and when you find your lover, give them an email address from that domain. This way you control access. If you are not doing anything illegal, you won't have to worry about the emails being subpoenaed. Also never, never, never send a compromising photo of yourself digitally that is plain old stupid. One of the problems now is people are uploading the candid Polaroid's.

Some great words from my man Sun Tzu "**To ... not prepare is the greatest of crimes; to be prepared beforehand for any contingency is the greatest of virtues.**"

Chapter 17
Everybody Lies

Before I go on my rant about politicians and how they are mostly a bunch of lying pricks, I want to put my shit on the table. I am far from the perfect citizen or close to being a good American. I have always walked my own road, and that road has involved a mug shot or two, tax audits, infidelity and ruining a few people's lives in the process. The difference between me and a politician is that I don't stand on a soap box and sell snake oil. Like Popeye, I am what I am, which is a guy who wants to make the greatest amount of money in life, pay the lowest amount in taxes and have an apartment on Park Avenue in New York, one in Paris and perhaps an ocean-facing condo in the Cayman Islands. A man's got to have a dream!

"I have previously stated and I repeat now that the United States intends no military intervention in Cuba." John F. Kennedy, April 18, 1961 – Bay of Pigs

I would say I draw my opinions specifically from my own personal experiences, and I feel that I have had quite a variety of experiences. One of the most important lessons I have walked away with in life is that most people's lies and bullshit make the world go round. Which leads to the thought that most politicians lie and most campaigns are built on empty promises armed with an arsenal of Benjamin's, be it teachers, lawyers, governors, husbands, wives, priests, Chinese restaurant owners, mortgage brokers, prosecutors, judges, skip tracers and even authors. Lying makes the world go round.

I may sound cynical, but I do try to keep a balanced perspective in my thoughts about society and government. I am a hardcore liberal who would like to believe in the idea of American freedom, but I do not, because in truth this is not the land of milk and honey. Think about it--all basic necessities to survive cost money, like water, electricity, shelter, health care, medicine, and even food like milk and honey. We are sold a promise that we can grow up to be anything we choose to be, but it's bullshit. I can tell you one thing, for sure--I never would have become a professional liar, although I did want to be a jewel thief because being President was out of my reach. It's unfortunate, but it seems like the American dream is more about a bill of goods than a Bill of Rights.

"I am not a crook." – President Richard M. Nixon – Watergate

We, as citizens of this nation and other nations, should be aware and always question the actions of those who rule us. Most of all, we should never blindly trust those who represent the Seal of the Nation. I do believe that laws must be enforced to maintain a reasonable amount of social control, but I do not believe there should be total social control of information. Just because the information is there, it does not mean it should be offered to Big Brother and his associates to determine the anticipation of crime.

"In spite of the wildly speculative and false stories of arms for hostages and alleged ransom payments, we did not-—repeat, did not-—trade weapons or anything else for hostages, nor will we." Ronald Reagan - Iran-Contra Affair

What I am getting at is the invasive collecting of information. Again, we should never trust Big Brother one hundred percent, but the reality is that law enforcement needs and should have access to information and data. I personally think certain profiling blurs the lines of investigations and too often narrow's the scope of truth. It's like the THOUGHT POLICE.

"It is the job of the Thought Police to uncover and punish thought-crime and thought-criminals, using psychology and omnipresent surveillance from telescreens to find and eliminate members of society who were capable of the mere thought of challenging ruling authority." George Orwell - Nineteen Eighty-Four

Let me introduce to you John Poindexter. John Poindexter had an impressive military career, rising to the rank of Vice Admiral and also serving in the military branch of the government as Deputy National Security Advisor and National Security Advisor. He was also indicted and convicted for his involvement in the Iran-Contra Affair, a scandal that covertly facilitated arms sales to Iran during the Reagan administration. His conviction was reversed on appeal.

THE PLAYERS
OLIVER NORTH – CONVICTION REVERSED
JOHN POINDEXTER – CONVICTION REVERSED
CASPER WEINBERGER - PARDONED
WILLIAM CASEY – INCAPABLE OF TESTIFYING
ROBERT C. MCFARLANE - PARDONED
ELLIOT ABRAMS - PARDONED
ALAN D. FIERS - PARDONED
CLAIR GEORGE - PARDONED
DUANE CLARRIDGE - PARDONED
RICHARD V. SECORD - CONVICTION EXPUNGED
ALBERT HAKIM – PROBATION

My initial point here is these motherfuckers lie to forward

their own agenda so you should not have too much guilt about lying to protect your information.

Why am I telling you about John Poindexter? Simply, he played a major part in TIA, Total Information Awareness, which was--and may still secretly be--a hard-core Big Brother plan that would have collected every piece of information and dumped it into a database to create profiles of US citizens. Imagine your bank records, credit card purchases, movie rentals, IP addresses, email addresses, phone records, utility bills and usage, pizza delivery records, VFW records, American Legion records, chess club membership, porn downloads and the whole shebang being collected and sent to a government database, all for the protection of "the American way".

Let me digress a moment, because it's important that you understand that I do believe that law enforcement should have access to information. For example, I am all for body scanners before getting on a plane. I have no problem with standing in a machine with my arms raised like a criminal while the machine makes its grinding sound and does its thing. I know I am not going to blow up or hijack a plane, but I do not know about the stranger next to me, be he black, white, Chinese or Muslim. Therefore, I want that person sitting next to me to be fully scanned, probed and cleared for takeoff and for that to happen I am willing to give up some privacy. I actually said this on a blog radio show hosted by some paranoid conspiracy hack of a host. The host was shocked. Her attitude was, How could I believe in privacy and consider such scanning acceptable? My answer was simple--I do not want to blow up into a million little pieces. What's so hard to understand about that? Therefore I suggest the TSA scan and probe all.

"A few months ago, I told the American people I did not trade

arms for hostages. My heart and my best intentions still tell me that's true, but the facts and evidence tell me it is not." President Ronald Reagan, admitting the Iran-Contra Affair, March 1987

Back to Total Information Awareness. I do not see how a system like this would help save the country from disaster. To a former information thief like myself this system would be a great place to obtain information. Let's face it, in the beginning it might have been used for some idealistic good, but eventually its uses would have made their way into the hands of any law enforcement agent in the name of fighting terrorism. What I have come to learn in the information business is that sources can be bought! Sometimes that source is a local cop, big city detective, state police officer, or perhaps just some broke-ass government worker needing a new pair of shoes.

While you are creating and sharing your Digital DNA, do keep the idea of TIA in the back of your head and realize that it is possible that your online information is being extracted by some government geek. Forget possible. It is happening. I believe in the idea of protecting the country, but I do not think my Netflix account or dirty text messages to my girlfriend are a matter of national safety, and honestly, they are nobody's fucking business but my own. Unfortunately, that just aint the way society works in this digital dystopia.

"Read my lips: no new taxes." George H.W. Bush, before his election as President.

The interesting thought about this type of intrusive surveillance is that it's not based on traditional law enforcement methods of investigating wrongdoing. What it does is investigate everyone and determine if someone is capable of doing wrong. So much for the "innocent until proven guilty" way of investigating crimes.

One of the humorous parts, or maybe the truly sad part about this evil concoction known as TIA, was the guy helming it, John Poindexter, who stated that it was his duty to withhold information from the Congress in reference to the Iran-Contra affair, and who was convicted on several counts of conspiracy. Feeling safe? Keep working that Digital DNA and posting those tweets, blogs and whatever comes next in the social network playground.

"I want you to listen to me. I'm going to say this again: I did not have sexual relations with that woman, Miss Lewinsky."
President Bill Clinton

TIA did not become an authorized program. Amazing! Some of those people working for Big Brother actually said no. Whether it was a budget issue or issues of intrusion, who cares? Because no matter how you look at it, TIA just means Taking It All. Then again, Big Brother lies, and perhaps TIA is now just a horse of another color hidden in a different type of invasive software.

"Weapons of Mass Destruction" President George W. Bush

As Howard Stern would say "Here's the dillio" we are being lied to constantly by our government, our employees if you will. I say lie to protect your information online, just like a snake in the grass.

Chapter 18
Digital Distortion

Digital Distortion is the act of building websites that have POSITIVE, NEUTRAL and NEGATIVE ATTRIBUTED information and that compete with sites that display information about you.

POSITIVE
FRANK M. AHEARN OF VENICE BEACH, CA, SHOWED REMORSE FOR/ABOUT THE YEARS OF LYING.

NEUTRAL
FRANK M. AHEARN OF VENICE BEACH, CA, DID NOT LIE.

NEGATIVE ATTRIBUTED
HANK N. AHEARN (distorted name and city) OF REDONDO BEACH, CA, SHOWED NO REMORSE ABOUT THE YEARS OF LYING.

If www.FrankAhearn.**COM** has negative information about you, you will purchase the same domain name with a different extension, like www.FrankAhearn.**NET**. Essentially, you strip out the negative information about yourself and replace it with positive or neutral information, while attributing negative information to a distorted name similar to your own.

For those of you who do not know what a domain or extension is, a domain is the name of the website, and the extension is the com, net, biz or info at the end of the domain name.

At this point I am assuming you have already searched out your Digital DNA and separated the sites into positive, negative and neutral categories. If not, you need to go back to the Digital DNA chapter and locate the information known about you.

Let's start with the negative information you've located and assume you have been unsuccessful at politely asking or pretexting the websites to get rid of this negative information. You need to search sites like networksolutions.com or godaddy.com to find out if you can buy the same domain name with different ex-tensions.

IMPORTANT

Purchase all domains for one year via a prepaid credit card, and dump the credit card when the operation is complete. Make the domain name a private registration with bogus WHOIS information, or keep it public but make sure it has no connection to you.

LET THE DISTORTION BEGIN

It is possible that doing this could run into copyright issues because the content may be owned by a newspaper or some blog moron who doesn't really give a shit about your information. You, too, shouldn't give a shit because this is total war, and we are taking no prisoners. Once you build the sites and they are published, you walk away from them and let them exist in digital dystopia, and let the content owner try to figure out who posted the sites and information. In the great words of Frank M. Ahearn, "Fuck those bastards!" As you can see I like that line.

On your distortion site there are several types of distortions you want to create, and the website you purchased will give you at least a thousand pages. So begin thinking of POSITIVE, NEUTRAL AND NEGATIVE ATTRIBUTIONS.

POSITIVE
FRANK M. AHEARN OF VENICE BEACH, CA, SHOWED REMORSE ABOUT THE YEARS OF LYING. (yeah right!)

This would be positive if the articles posted online about me stated that Frank M. Ahearn has no remorse about lying for a living.

NEUTRAL
FRANK M. AHEARN OF REDONDO BEACH, CA, SHOWED REMORSE FOR/ABOUT THE YEARS OF LYING.

The website you build would have content like Frank M. Ahearn did not lie for a living.

NEGATIVE ATTRIBUTED
HANK N. AHEARN (distorted name) OF REDONDO BEACH, CA, SHOWED NO REMORSE ABOUT THE YEARS OF LYING.

This type of site is applying the negative information to someone else by deviating your name and other type of identifiers.

We begin with stripping the NEGATIVE information from websites and filling in positive information.

POSITIVE DISTORTION
The idea is to take sentences like "John Smith of Cleveland showed no remorse when he admitted to outsourcing his

company's customer service department." Change it to "John Smith of Cleveland showed total remorse when he was forced to outsource his customer service department." Load this type of articles to blogs and websites you build.

Do not do this on just one page of your site; take the same content and do it on all fifty pages of the distortion site.

POSITIVE
Frank the drunk to Frank the hunk
Frank the thief to Frank the great

I really enjoy creating deception.

NEUTRAL INFORMATION
Neutral information is identifiers other than your name. "John Gault of Cleveland showed no remorse when he admitted to outsourcing his company's customer service department." Change Cleveland to Toledo or Salt Lake City. Create a bunch of neutral pages changing the city, your age, spouse name and anything else that is a non-name identifier.

NEUTRAL
Chicago to Newark
Harvard to Princeton
Thirty-Eight to Forty-Four
Balding to Dreads

NEGATIVE ATTRIBUTED
On your distortion site you are going to attribute the negative information to a name similar to yours.

Take, for example, "John Smith showed no remorse when he admitted to outsourcing his company's customer service department." Change the name like this: "John Smyth showed no remorse when he admitted to outsourcing his company's customer service department." This way people who know you may believe it is someone else. It is important to hit all identifiers like city, company name and so on.

DISTORT YOUR NAME
Ahearn
Ahearne
Ahern
Ohearn
Ahearnia
Hayhearn
Ahearnia (like they called me in school)

A good tool to use is if your name is the same as a B-list celebrity use their name.

On the negative attributed pages, you can also change the negative to positive information, as well as change the neutral information, and the distortion of your name should be on several pages.

Do not make a massive number of changes on one page. The goal is to change the information slightly so when a searcher puts your information into a search engine, they will find your distortion sites with slightly changed information. This does not guarantee that the searcher will not find the original site with the negative information. What it does do, however, is greatly increase the odds that a searcher will come across the distorted pages and utilize that information.

If the negative website shows an identifier like city, town or state, you need to distort that identifier. For example, change "Frank Tromper of Detroit" to "Frank Tromper of Des Moines," and so on. On another page, create "Frank Trompe of Des Moines," dropping a letter at the end of the name.

Since you have at least a thousand pages to spare on one domain name, you need to take utilize that digital real estate and keep on distorting.

You can also copy random pages from the negative site and post them on your distortion site to give it more fill. Also, set up accounts with various advertising sites so you can post advertising like Google ads or even Amazon ads. Who knows? Maybe you will make some money. However, if you do put ads on the domains, you can be traced that way if you set up direct deposit. So maybe placing the ads is a good idea, but not actually collecting the money. Maybe you could have the revenue sent to your favorite charity.

TYPES OF DIGITAL DISTORTION

Negative Words to Positive Words
Negative Sentences to Positive Sentences
Name Distortion
Geographical Distortion
Copy Random Pages
Add Advertising Ads
False Flags

FALSE FLAGS

False flags are designed to deceive the public in such a way that the operations appear as though they are being carried out by other entities.

Do not put contact information on websites or blogs!

I have my own idea of what a False Flag should be, and that is taking news article or blog stories and stripping out the real subjects' names and putting YOUR name in the article. Search out the blandest and silliest articles that have nothing to do with anything about you and utilize them to plant fake flags.

There are thousands of blogs that focus on only certain categories, like fish or Wyoming, so the idea is to have a five-hundred-page website or blog all about your name. Keep in mind that you are doing this to your name, not necessarily you, so do not feel funny about the content or limit the categories because they are not smart, cool or fancy enough for you. You are building sites to defend yourself, not make yourself look cool. The purpose of Digital Distortion is to battle information. When you move on to Digital Identities, that will be about battling your name and creating fake names to take credit for the negative.

Chapter 19
Packing Lies

Packing Lies is a tool I use that copies, pastes and deviates search engine information onto prebuilt deception websites. When you type information into a search engine a list of websites links with a reduced descriptions display and allow to click and follow thru to the web page. This is how individuals searching out your information discover the goods.

EXAMPLE OF SEARCH ENGINE RESULTS

Frank M. Ahearn - How to Disappear (excellent book)
www.frankahearn.com
The leader in teaching people how to disappear, for over twenty years Frank M. Ahearn has been considered one of the leading skip tracers in the world.

Let's assume that search results display:
Frank M. Ahearn - How to Disappear
www.frankahearn.com
For over twenty years Frank M. Ahearn has been ripping people off left and right with his online scams.

What you need to do is copy every negative result known about you online. When you have that complete, buy domain names that sound as if they are news websites. Grab names like The Real News, American News Information, France Hot Topics, and Germany Speaks. The idea is to build a website that appears as if it grabs news headlines from around the world.

Original Results

Frank M. Ahearn - How to Disappear
www.frankahearn.com
For over twenty years Frank M. Ahearn has been ripping people off left and right with his online scams.

You are going to paste the original link information you copied from search engines, but you are going to deviate the information in your favor.

Deviated Results
Frank M. Ahearn - How to Disappear
www.frankahearn.com
For over twenty years Frank M. Ahearn has been assisting people left and right with his online services.

Let's assume the negative information about you is about a bad divorce. You want to grab other headlines about divorce. Build the site with cases about famous people getting divorced, divorce lawyers and such. Grab positive headlines that share your name, like "Rev. Ahearn retires after writing How to Deceive." Put several headlines about yourself on each page, and fill the pages with tons of other information. Do not just add headlines, but put news widgets on the site, such as calendars and weather widgets. Also, put links to charitable websites and other types of links, as if your site is making money via the link advertising.

The great part here is that you can buy a domain name for ten dollars, make it private for nine bucks, and set up a hosting package for a hundred bucks a year with the availability of $9.99 pages.

You spend your time copying and pasting from news sites all around the world and you load up your pack of lies website with real information and your changed information. This takes a lot of effort, but it works. Your next step is building **SINGLE SITES** to link.

Do not forget: make sure you cannot be connected to the websites and the websites cannot be connected to you.

Chapter 20
Single Sites

You also want to target specific websites and blogs that have damaging articles about you by building SINGLE SITES. Single sites are one-page websites you build that look as if they are local news sources. You are going to rewrite the negative articles and make them positive.

This structure is similar to building your pack of lies websites. Keep in mind that appearance is important, so make them appear real.

You want to use the same name or a similar name to that of the enemy website. Therefore, if the enemy site is "NewYorkDailyWords," you want to buy and build:

NewYorkDailyWordsBlog
NewYorkDailyWordsUpdatePage
BlogNewYorkDailyWords

Keep in mind--your new sites should be similar, but not exactly the same, so you do not encounter any copyright issues. Isn't that funny? The enemy can post anything about you and it is copyright-protected, but you need to be careful, even if you are the subject of the article! When you design your site, think local. For instance, put up a map of Nebraska as the logo, or, if it's a UK newspaper, pop a crown on the site. The best place to get content is from the news or blog site itself.

If you build the sites correctly by using proper keywords and descriptions, the sites will rise to the top of search engines. Therefore, it is wise to learn a little about SEO, search engine optimization.

Single sites are one-page stand-alone websites that resemble a site that has negative information about people. The goal is for your site to be similar in name and resemble the website in font, color and description. What I have done in the past is place a banner ad with a link to a newspaper site; therefore, if someone stumbles on the single site, they click on the banner and next thing you know, they are at the actual newspaper website. I also copy online ads and place them on my websites, including the link to the advertisers.

Chapter 21
Phone Hackers, Inc.

Phone hacking has become a popular digital sport, in which a hacker of sorts gets into a person's smart phone and extracts the photos, text and emails and then releases them online. At the time I am writing this book, Scarlett Johansson has been the recent victim of such a hack. Unfortunately for her, there were a few photos she did not want others to see, and now they are all over the Internet-—forever! This is an article I wrote for Spectator Magazine in the UK:

From Spectator Magazine, 27th August 2011- The dark art of stealing personal information is not confined to newspapers, as a former practitioner explains...

'Hi, this is Mr Pretext from Mobile Phone Activations. Our systems are down and I need you to bring up a customer's mobile account for me, please.' I must have repeated this lie thousands of times in the past 20 years. It helped me gain access to information-—criminal records, Social Security numbers, phone logs —-that I would then hand on to all sorts of clients: journalists, insurers, cuckolded husbands and even policemen. As an American who spent many years in this underground industry, I can tell you that the British phone-hacking scandal has exposed only a tiny part of a vast criminal network.

In the old days, private investigators would peer through letterboxes or ransack the bins of their targets. In the past ten to fifteen years, however, technology has multiplied the ways in which people like me can snoop on people like you.

Mobile phone records, health records, anything that is held digitally, can be accessed. My working day would start with a request to find the phone records of one person, or the bank statement of another, or maybe the criminal record of a third. I'd find private details through utility companies, shops or frequent-flyer schemes. Then I'd pick up the phone and start blagging, or, as we called it in my part of the trade, pretexting: lying to extract personal details.

Then I yanked open a drawer full of prepaid mobile phones and calling cards. Glenn Mulcaire, the man at the centre of the News of the World case, was a professional footballer before he became an investigator. If that surprises you, it shouldn't. What I did for a living--and what detectives acting for tabloid journalists are alleged to have done for a living--was hardly technical. It's not hacking, in the sense of requiring computer programming skills or sophisticated manipulation of telecom systems. All I needed was the ability to lie convincingly. The tactics uncovered in the News of the World case--accessing voicemail by giving a default code, or sometimes by persuading someone to set a code of your choice --are standard operating procedure for those on the underground superhighway of private information for sale.

Our gift was the ability to convince other people to give us the information we needed. Hacking phone systems is no trouble at all when you have a contact in the phone company or the police. I'd call the telephone company, posing as my target. 'I lost my bill and need to take a few minutes and go over my list of calls,' I'd say. Some people agreed straightaway, others wouldn't. When I felt the operator was on the fence, I played the sympathy card. 'If I don't turn in my expenses to my boss, he won't reimburse me,' I'd say, or explain haltingly the surprise trip to Legoland I was planning for my children. The trick then was to stay silent. You'd be amazed just how much information could be spilled--after an awkward pause, of course--using these simple techniques.

I called my trade "skip-tracing," not "hacking." I was paid to find criminals, defaulting debtors and court witnesses. I carried out work *for newspapers, too. When they wanted to talk to some children who had spent the night with Michael Jackson at Neverland, they called me. When they wanted to monitor O.J. Simpson's bank accounts, they called me. I was once hired by a paparazzo to find Ozzy Osbourne's private telephone numbers. I found eight. Accessing messages on a person's mobile phone was just one of the services we offered, but it was the least requested. I would not listen to the messages. Usually my clients just wanted the voicemail passcode, so they had the pleasure of listening in themselves. The most useful information, the stuff that earned me the big money, was detailed lists of calls from mobile phones. They were surprisingly easy to acquire. All it took was a simple call to a mobile phone company. I'd be asked for basic security, such as an address, date of birth and perhaps a password. Often, the person paying me already had that information. If not, it took just a little more pretexting to obtain it.*

The information black market really boomed around 2000, when all manner of companies began putting their bills online, and accessing them therefore became easier. It doesn't matter if you bank with RBS in Scotland or Banca d'Italia in Rome. Online services make it easier to access anything, anywhere.

It took time for the law to catch up. Until the 1990s, many of my trade's techniques weren't specifically illegal. And about ten years ago, some were punished with a caution or a fine. Now it's prison sentences--as a number of journalists in Britain may find out. What is regarded as an outright crime now was, a decade ago, more of a grey area, both in America and Britain. My clients suspected I used murky techniques, but not necessarily illegal ones. A lot of the time, they were right.

That said, I tried to set my own limits. If you were on my list, then I believed that you'd done something stupid or illegal--or at least that you had chosen to forgo privacy by entering showbiz.

I'd like to say that I left the skip-tracing industry because of a crisis of conscience, but the truth is that it was getting too dangerous. It seemed as if every day another law was passed against one of my tricks. My decision to retire was made when I heard a helicopter over my New Jersey office. I threw a laptop to the ground and started stamping on it, and flung everything into a canal. I destroyed, in all, about $5,000 worth of equipment. As it turned out, the helicopter belonged to park police, who were searching the canal for a lost sea cow.

I don't know how long Mulcaire was in my old business, but obviously he should have got out sooner. Or at the very least, he should have observed its golden rule: once the information has gone to the client, erase all traces of the transaction. I don't understand why he kept it all, or how the police ended up with 11,000 pages of evidence and 4,000 mobile phone numbers. Perhaps he wanted to write a book. Perhaps he was stupid. Perhaps he hadn't realised how the law had caught up with our trade.

For my part, I have turned from poacher to gamekeeper. I now advise people on how to hide from private investigators and skip-tracers. There is a growing market for this service. People are realising how vulnerable they are to identity theft. Companies are buying, selling and trading information all the time. The deals that bring you junk mail today may lead to identity theft and financial ruin tomorrow. Do you really want your contact information, private details and family connections splashed all over the Internet? It doesn't take a genius to start harvesting and selling this information.

Newspapers may be forced to start behaving themselves in Britain, but that will not end invasions of privacy. Skip-tracing will exist as long as we have lawyers, criminals and cheating spouses--and personal information which is held by businesses that have no idea how to protect it. The black market for private data is huge, growing and global. Some newspapermen may be imprisoned, but skip-tracing and phone-hacking will be with us for some time to come.

I find the article a little funny because it has that Brit editing to it and it is somewhat out of my voice. I think the overall idea is that there are skip tracers, private investigators, journalists and others who do what they have to do to get your information.

Phone hacking can happen in a few different ways, and it also encompasses several meanings. For instance, in the article I do not really consider this phone hacking, but what was done to Scarlett Johansson is more in the realm of phone hacking than what the UK newspaper did. Either way, they are intrusions you need to protect yourself from.

TYPES OF INTRUSION
Obtaining Phone Records
Obtaining Voice Messages
Accessing GPS Location
Obtaining Text Messages
Obtaining Photos
Obtaining Videos

There are two ways to access and listen to your cell phone voice messages. One is to dial an access number and enter a password or dial the same number; if calling from your own cell phone, no password is required and the messages are read. **IMPORTANT**--if your cell phone is set up so that you do not request a password when dialing from the actual phone, you are **VULNERABLE**!

Software like Spoof Card (www.spoofcard.com) tricks out the caller ID on your cell or landline phone and allows you to enter any number you choose to be displayed on your caller ID when dialing out.

When a person uses a Spoof Card type software and enters your cell number to be displayed on the next call, if they call your phone, it will display your actual cell phone number, and if you do not answer the call and it rolls to your voice message system, it will read the number as you calling in from your actual cell phone and it will allow access to all of your voice mail messages. If by chance you see your own number showing up on your caller ID, you have problems.

Always use passwords on your cell phone!

Another type of breach in the cell phone world is cloning phones, where the person with a clone sees and hears every event that happens on your cell phone. This is really difficult to do and was more popular in the earlier days of cell phones.

In the Scarlett Johansson case, I believe the hacker obtained what was currently on her cell phone at that particular time. A further breach would be hacking in and obtaining historical data?/a historical date on the cell phone, historical meaning every text, photo and email, the same as law enforcement would obtain with a subpoena. Even if Scarlett had deleted the current photos, it is possible that a hacker or really good skip tracer could access the historical data.

There is only one way to protect your privacy when it comes to the cellular world: Do not take or send compromising photos, and do not send compromising texts or emails. If you do, erase them immediately from your phone. Do note that those compromising bits and bites are still available when needed by law enforcement.

Back in the Stone Age we had to bring the film from our camera to get developed so we could enjoy our photos. I have heard many stories of people dropping off a roll of film whose contents are topless photos of the wife. The next thing you know the photos have been passed around town. There is no difference between the moron in the Photomat booth and the geek in the back office of your cellular carrier.

DO NOT PLAY DIRTY ON YOUR CELL PHONE – IT NEVER, EVER GOES AWAY!

Chapter 22
Electric Serve, E-DISCO & Landlocked

What you do online can and will be used against you in more ways than one. I know some people have the attitude that if you do nothing wrong, you have nothing to worry about. Well, I say bullshit to that. In the Digital DNA chapter I stated that when something new is introduced in society, eventually someone down the road finds new uses for that thing. In the digital realm, it's some techie who comes up with a bright idea of utilizing that information for profit, and then Big Brother uses it for control. In our current society, information is probably the most important commodity. Without information there would be no Internet as we know it. There would probably be only a world of images and games.

This chapter is really an important one, and paying attention to what I write here can save you heartache, embarrassment, and money, and assist you in maintaining a little worldly freedom. Just like you must maintain a sense of responsibility in your home and work life you must do so in your third life — the digital.

WE NOW HAVE THREE LIVES
First Life – Home
Second Life – Work
Third Life – Digital

If you are living your third life without care and leaving digital trails, electronic footprints, comments, photos, blogs, or Tweets, or sending compromising emails, sexting, or Friending without any afterthought of how it can affect you,

you've got some problems. Always think of three terms when you are using a cell phone, laptop or other type of device that transmits information. The terms are Electric Serve, E-DISCO and Landlocked.

Our third life, the digital, the online is becoming somewhat more important than our actual physical life and is close to the point where it stands proxy for who we are. This chapter will show you how society is looking beyond us, our physical selves, looking directly at our digital life. It is as if we humans could be replaced by our digital selves.

THE CAVEMAN DAYS OF SERVING PAPERS

Back in my days of skip tracing, I used to do some extreme process serving. For those of you not familiar with service of process, it is a requirement or formal invitation by the court for someone to show up and be part of a case. The person could be a defendant being sued, or a witness in a case. Typically a process server shows up at the front door and hands the subject the legal summons to appear. You've been served. Not every service of process is so simple, and a few times I have been called in to figure out a ruse to serve a difficult subject. Most people do not like to be served and rather now show up in court.

I believe I am watching technology strip us of all human elements and we are soon to be identified only by our Social Security number, email address, domain name and social networking identity. Perhaps it's just modernity, and privacy consultants need not apply.

As I said before some of us prefer not to go to court, whether as a defendant or a witness. Both suck and spending the day in court is simply a waste of time unless you're a lawyer overcharging a client. Let me clarify: if you're a lawyer, going to court you are making money. It is the opportunity to charge an outrageous amount of money and be a hired gun. Truth and justice have been replaced by billable hours.

LAWYERS SUCK!

What some US states are now doing, and others considering, is to allow service of process on a person's social media accounts.

Utah Courts
Even though you cannot find the person to be served, you may know where they accept communications: email; mail to a friend or relative; a social network, such as Facebook; a text number or phone number, or a Twitter name. With the court's permission, you might be able to send the complaint and summons directly to the person by mail, email or social media.

It is mind-blowing that the legal system would even consider this route of service. If I were going to sue a person but could not locate them (highly unlikely), I would build a bunch of social media in the name of the person I was trying to sue and serve them through those media. If the person I was suing did not respond, I could possibly win the suit by default because they never showed up in court or answered the summons. This is totally illegal, but not everyone plays by the rules.

If you are being sued, what you need to think about is shutting down your social media, changing your email address or setting up an auto-responder claiming you have moved to Zimbabwe and no longer participate in the digital world.

Through research, I located several cases where a lawyer was able to serve process on a corporation via telex machine or email. One such serve was to the WHOIS on a corporation's domain name. In one of the cases I read about, the court demanded that proof be shown that the subject who opened the email had viewed the notice.

From Federal Courts Law Review

"A simple and free service known as SpyPig offers instant verification of receipt. The sender writes the email in HTML format and inserts a picture or blank image hosted at a SpyPig server. When the recipient opens the HTML-formatted message, the image is loaded from the server, and the logs of the server will reflect when the image was loaded. This creates a record of when the email was opened. SpyPig then notifies the sender that the email has been opened."

www.spypig.com

I am not going to bore you with a bunch of examples of how people were served via technology, but I am going to say that this is the future, like it or not. No one ever expects to be sued or be part of a legal case. Sometimes shit just happens.

AGAIN SOMETIMES SHIT HAPPENS!

In the offshore world of expatriates there's a philosophy known as the Five Flag and Three Flag theories.

FIVE FLAGS
1. Passport and Citizenship – in a country that does not tax money earned outside the country or control actions.
2. Legal Residence – in a tax haven.

3. Business Base – where you earn your money, ideally somewhere with low corporate tax rates.

4. Asset Haven – where you keep your money, ideally somewhere with low taxation of savings interest and capital gains.

5. Playgrounds – where you spend your money, ideally somewhere with low consumption tax and VAT.

THREE FLAGS
1. Have your citizenship somewhere that does not tax income earned outside the country.
2. Have your businesses and speculations in stable, low- or no-tax countries.
3. Live as a tourist in countries where what you do for a living is valued, not outlawed.

You need to think of the digital world as an offshore haven and embrace certain philosophies that are designed to protect your information. I do not mean the personal information I dealt with in "How to Disappear," but the information that connects you to your third life, which, again, is your digital world.

In my physical life I have only two things in my name, my bank account and my cell phone. My bank account is all online, and I do not receive any statements. When there are communications from my bank, I use as my address? Chateau Marmont in West Hollywood, Attention Penthouse B, for bullshit. My cell phone has online billing, and all communication goes to Fenway Park. My domains are under my name, but I change the WHOIS information quite frequently.

After I finally got rid of most of the skip tracing company and there were only myself and two other employees, I created a fictional office manager named Jane. If there were any issues, problems or mistakes, I blamed them on Jane. You should consider creating a fictional partner in your online business and let that virtual entity be the face or name identity of the company. I do not think one should defraud, but it can't hurt to have your virtual partner taking the heat in unwanted or embarrassing situations.

If you need an online presence for business, I suggest you carefully evaluate how the information you put up in the digital world can be connected to you. Also, think about an exit plan if you had to shut down today. Perhaps have a second website built that is hosted in a different country but not published as a backup business entity.

THINK
Am I vulnerable because of online information?
Are my personal and business lives connected?

What if I need to shut down? Can I start back up in an hour? Think of your digital world the way one thinks of doing business offshore.

Electronic Discovery, better known as E-DISCO, refers to discovery in civil litigation: which is the exchange of information in electronic format. If you are involved in a legal case and E-DISCO is requested by a lawyer or prosecutor, it pretty much means everything you have done via cell phone or online can and will be converted to paper form for use in the case.

E-DISCO, aka LITIGATION SUPPORT
Text Messages
Voice mail Messages

Email Messages
Photo Messages
Instant Messages
Video Communication

Also EDISCO is only one part of a civil or criminal case, financial records, health records and anything else a lawyer or prosecutor can whip up to expose your life.

I believe many of us would be concerned if the world got to see our digital skeletons. When I text my mother, I look like a saint, but when I text a friend, I could be viewed as a vile, unsympathetic madman with no concern for the human race. Do note that my mother taught me when I was young never to write something down that I would ever be embarrassed about—-something to think about from Momma Ahearn.

If this was my 125,000-word manifesto about deceiving, I would have shared more cases of E-DISCO, but what's the point? Just keep the mindset that what you say, text and email can and will be used against you, not only in a court of law but for the entire world to see, and for eternity!

LANDLOCKED--CLOSED IN BY LAND

One afternoon I was listening to the radio, and the news reported that radio host Michael Savage was denied entry to the UK because of his inflammatory mouth. This got me to wondering who else was denied entry into the UK and other countries. Martha Stewart was denied entry into the UK because of her felony conviction, which, when broken down, was only a stupid lie. Unfortunately, you cannot lie to law enforcement, but do note--they can lie to you.

Sometimes I am a little paranoid, which leads me to wonder what would or could happen if customs in another country misconstrued what I do for a living. Years ago the Bank of Montreal froze all of my accounts because of my original "How to Disappear" article. That was a pain in the ass. I couldn't imagine not being allowed into a country because of what I do for a living or my personal thoughts about freedom. By the way the bank froze my assets because I used their name in the article and they assumed I was giving an example about money laundering through their bank.

If you write a blog that could be considered inflammatory or offer a service that dwells in a legal gray area, you, too, could be denied entry into a country. A cousin of a friend of mine came to the US via France and he was detained in customs for about two hours. My friend asked my opinion and I popped his name into Google and, sure enough, he wrote a somewhat radical blog about French politics and referred to himself as a militant. If you consider yourself a militant, assume that customs just may treat you like one.

If you have a blog that is somewhat radical, you need to evaluate the weight it carries when you go through customs. Even if your blog is not radical, but if offensive to another country, like saying the Queen looks like John Lithgow or all French cheese smells like dirty feet, a country may and can refuse you entry. They can turn you back for the smallest reasons or no reason at all.

You need to evaluate your digital life and question if there is information that can make you landlocked. There is no doubt that customs in most countries have some software that searches the web and extracts information about foreigners landing on their soil. It's possible that you can walk to the customs counter and the agent will ask if you are the person who writes the blog titled "The Saudi Prince is a Bitch." Well, you can figure out what happens next.

Having your say online is what graffiti artists have been doing all along in society. They put up big pieces in color or only simple tags, just to let people know they were there. The goal in writing graffiti is to be the most popular and not be identified as the one who sprayed or marked the wall. Think of your blog or digital life as online graffiti. Get it out there, but do not let anyone know it is you behind the name.

Gunz 207 was here...

Chapter 23
Think Security

The world is becoming smaller. We hear it all the time. In reality, the world is not getting smaller, but access to information is becoming greater. '

Frank Tromper, a businessman, was sitting in a hotel lounge in Mozambique when he got into a conversation with a stranger. Frank, a savvy businessman and seasoned traveler, knew what to discuss and what not to discuss while in a foreign country.

The mysterious stranger spoke about business, travel and his own personal adventures, but then he mentioned the town of Scarsdale, New York. Frank freaked because that is where he lives, and it was too much of a coincidence. He excused himself, went to his room, gathered all of his belongings and left the hotel without checking out. The big question was whether the conversation was a fluke or whether a possible abduction was being planned.

An employee of the hotel searched Frank Tromper's home address, which was provided when the reservation was made with his credit card. The employee of the hotel searched a free website that revealed the value of his home — four million dollars.

No offense to those in Mozambique, but the average yearly income there is $370, which makes a Frank Tromper a viable candidate for abduction in such a country.

The real estate search can also work in reverse. I could pop your address into a site and find your home's value and then search your name in a free site like www.ZabaSearch.com and match up your address and locate potential family members like spouse or children. While you are in a foreign county, a criminal can grab a family member. I am not trying to be an alarmist, but rather to exhibit how information can be used in a dangerous way.

I find it surprising that companies post photos with the bios of key executives in the corporation. If you travel for business and your information is easily accessible online, you should consider creating some fake travel identities. **No, not a bogus passport.** Think about it. Why travel with a business credit card that identifies you as the Sr. Vice President of CEO of a Fortune 500 company? Sure, prestige is cool, but being tied up in a mud hut is not. I suggest you build a Fake Digital Identity type website using your name and make it a profession you can identify with. If you are an avid fisherman or cupcake baker why not travel as if you are selling fishing or cupcake services as opposed to a five-hundred-million-dollar hedge fund. The answer is simple executives put prestige and ego before safety and security.

My client Frank Tromper decided it was best he no longer travel as the high powered executive. I built him a websites that displays the profession of a photographer.

www.FrankTromper.info

HOME: Welcome to my website. I have been a travel photographer for ten years.

ABOUT: I have been living in [this lower middle class city] for ten years, and I am single.

SERVICES: I travel and take photos for nonprofit companies-- no money in that.

CONTACT: 212-555-1212 (Google this number.) 555 Madison Avenue, New York, NY 10001 (mail drop)

When you travel, use a credit card that matches the fake website name which will identify you as a photographer to anyone who snoops. Take business cards and a photo portfolio with you, and leave these in your hotel room for prying eyes. Your real business information, like contracts or research, can be shipped to a mail drop in that city.

Going backwards a moment I told you about the client who contacted me last year because they were planning a worldwide trip that included some less-than-desirable countries. I was asked to search out online information that could be associated with them and their wealth. The first piece of information I came across was campaign donations. There were loads of them, and they were beyond the amount donated by the average citizen. If we Google, so do criminals, and if they find your list of donations year after year, it will be obvious that you have a sizeable disposable income.

There was a time when you had to actually get up and go to a city or county hall of records to locate information. If it wasn't near you, then you had to find a person or service that was able to access the public record for you. Now it's all there for the world to see, even in Mozambique.

Prior to the Internet, we had a home life and a work life. The nature of the job you did determined how much of each life flowed into the other. If you were a cop, prosecutor or in another profession where you did not want the two worlds to meet, it was relatively easy to keep them apart. Now we have a third life, which is the digital life, which has minimal discretion and no hall monitor telling us what we should and should not do.

What if you were a prosecutor who has spent years putting criminals behind bars and now you are retired, enjoying life? What if that one guy was released from prison and decided to get some retribution and began searching your information online? No doubt there would be a newspaper article or two about you out there, as well as information from the bar exam and the address where you now practice law. What if the thug came across a newspaper article about your daughter getting married ten years ago, and from there located her on Facebook, which offered a spider web of family members? This may sound extreme, but it's all possible and happened to a client.

Again, I am not being an alarmist, but being realistic and demonstrating how your profession could put family members in harm's way. You should consider keeping both lives separate: maybe in your personal life all things are Frank Ahearn and maybe in your professional life all things are FM Ahearn. This is not an actual remedy, but sometimes it can blur the lines. Instruct all in your tribe never to post anything, including photos about you or what you do. And no matter what, never create an online connection to yourself.

So you're not the one putting people in jail, but you are someone who invented a widget worth ninety million dollars and are extremely proud of it.

Maybe your children are equally proud, and on their social networking site they have a photo of you and the article about the sale of the ninety-million-dollar widget. Being wealthy also means being a potential target. Be wise and take the value out of your children and caution them on family security.

Chapter 24
Fake Digital Identities

The chapter "Digital Distortion" combats negative information on websites. The first task is to buy up as many domain names as you can afford.

<u>DOMAIN NAMES</u>
FRANKAHEARN.COM
FRANKAHEARN.something
FRANKAHEARN.anything

<u>TRICK OUT YOUR NAME</u>
FRANKAHEARN
FRANKMAHEARN
FMAHEARN
AHEARNFRANK
FRANKIEAHEARN

Using Fake Digital Identities is a total war plan where you go all-out and attack your name. The objective is to create as many websites, blogs and social networking sites as possible using your name with a variety of content that is WORD-related or SENTENCE-related.

<u>WORD-RELATED</u>
DISAPPEAR
DECEIVE
SKIP TRACE
FIND
MISINFORMATION
DISINFORMATION

The plan is to have these Fake Digital Identities take credit for the information known about you and you do not want to be associated with. This tool is not only for negative information, but also for information that can make you and your family vulnerable.

A client contacted me because she was concerned about one piece of information that existed about her online. It was an article about her divorce where she obtained a windfall amount in the case. The newspaper article identified her with some background information about her children and this was a huge security concern.

The first goal was to create a blog about my client and how after she received her money she picked up and moved to Hawaii with her new husband Frank Tromper. So her name was no longer Stephanie Boney Bags but now Stephanie Tromper. I also posted photos not of her but an unknown family that claimed it was her, her new husband and children.

We also created other websites using different aspects of her life. For example, she went to school in Santa Fe, New Mexico, and so there is a blog from another fake identity that writes about all things Santa Fe, as well as websites that sell Santa Fe products. Now, if you pop the client's name into a search engine, there is an abundance of information available which assists in camouflaging the real client's looks and whereabouts.

For negative information online, let's say in your early days of business ventures you had a party planning business and it was not the greatest of services and you left a trail of unhappy customers. Via your damage control searching and Digital DNA, you locate there are some unpleasant articles and blogs about your unsuccessful and shitty a party planning business. Even worse, your name is connected to the negative information; however, you can be shielded by use of Fake Digital Identities.

THINK CONNECTIONS
LOCATION OF BUSINESS
BIO INFO
COLLEGE
HOMETOWN
SPOUSE NAME
CHILDREN NAMES
OTHER ASSOCIATED NAMES
PHOTOS
EMAIL ADDRESSES
PHONE NUMBERS

When you think of connections, search out nouns and separate them into people, places and things. (It's funny: looking back, I hated school and dropped out somewhere in the ninth grade. For the life of me, I never would have imagined that I would be telling others to identify nouns in paragraphs.) Try to be specific in identifying key words because this is the information that you will use to create the fake sites and assist in the deception.

PEOPLE
YOUR NAME
ASSOCIATES' NAMES
COMPANY NAME

When you begin buying your domain names, you should buy:

frankahearnpartyrentals.com
frankahearnbirthdayparties.com

If you are still in the city where the negative information appeared, you can give the Fake Digital Identities a presence in a different city by using a fake PO Box number as the address and a free Google number as the phone contact. On the fake website your fake digital identity can explain what happened with the other business and take full responsibility.

PLACES
MIAMI
DADE
COLLINS AVENUE
BROWARD

Build sites like Frankahearnmiami.com, which loves the Miami Dolphins, Miami Sound Machine, Miami Vice, Miami Boat Rentals, Tom Collins, and everything else connected to the place. Name Miami restaurants, Dade County businesses, and Broward County businesses. The idea is to go overboard.

THINGS
VIKING LOGO
'76 ELDORADO
OCEANFRONT OFFICE

Create websites using things as the contents, perhaps everything Viking. In the content of the sites, make sure to use your name. Say something like "HI, MY NAME IS FRANK AHEARN. I LOVE VIKING," or "FRANK AHEARN IS THE BIGGEST FAN OF 1976 ELDORADOS." It is important to put your name on the site, not just use it as a domain name this way it shows up in the search results.

<u>NEGATIVE WORDS</u>
IRRESPONSIBLE
FORGOT PARTY
DRINK
DIRTY
OVERPRICED
CHEAP
OLD SEATS

For the negative information, I would buy up sites like:

frankmahearndirtydrunk.com

Put up alcohol-related information, dirty dancing, and "I sell cheap goods," and make the site the bizarre rambling of an old wino. Keep in mind that when you create a website, you have the ability to build a thousand pages, so you can create a lot of fill.

<u>NEUTRAL</u>
BALLOONS
RIBBONS
CLOWN
PARTY FAVORS
BIRTHDAY
ANNIVERSARY
GRADUATION
INVITATIONS

MORE DOMAIN NAME EXAMPLES

FrankAhearn.com
FrankAhearnpartyPlanner.com
AhearnFrank.com
AhearnPartyPlanner.com
FrankAhearnBalloons.com

Build up the website with Google Ads, Amazon Ads and other links. Do not forget to include links on this site to your other party planning websites, and vice versa. For each website you build, you should create at least five social media sites. Do not limit yourself to the most well-known, like Facebook, MySpace or Twitter. However, sites like these are good places to begin your fake identities.

If you want to guarantee no one can figure out you are behind the websites instead of using your own ads copy and paste goggle ads from other websites and paste them on to you site. You can also download a banner ad or photo ad from a website and include the advertisers domain for the click through.

When you build the sites, think of a good bio, and give your fake identity a spouse. Pop a few kids into the scene, or the family dog. The more dimensional you create it, the more believable it will be to those who find the sites.

RECAP
Locate Websites & Blogs
Identify Who – What – Where – When
Identify People – Places – Things
Identify Negative Words
Identify Neutral Words
Purchase as Many Domains as Possible
Create Fake Digital Domains
Create Fake Social Network Sites

None of this is a piece of cake, and it is time-consuming. I guess you have to decide if the work is worth it in the long run. I use party planning as a template, but if you had a DUI, were part of a porn flick in college or had some other embarrassing or humiliating experience that is now available to others online, this concept can help you bury the real information.

If it's a DUI you got in Hackensack, New Jersey, you can create a blog and a fake digital identity who writes about DUI. This identity can admit to a past misdeed of drinking and driving in Hackensack, and by adding an identifier, can indicate somewhere on the site that he or she now lives in Bergenfield. It takes the spotlight away from you, and someone searching for that information will not necessarily be able to prove or disprove that it is you unless they pulled the actual arrest and that all depends on the state's availability of arrest information.

If you were one wild and crazy person in college and did that one-time porn flick under your real name, there is hope even for you. Build a website and make that fake identity a porn freak and take credit for the film. The hope here is that if your nemesis finds the film, they do not purchase it because they believe it's only a shared name. If they buy the film, that's another story.

The bottom line is that if you want to hide, bury or create online information confusion about yourself and your name, the only way is by Digital Distortion and Fake Digital Identities.

USE DISCRETION
- **OBTAIN PREPAID CREDIT CARDS**
- **PAY FOR ALL SITES ONE YEAR IN ADVANCE WITH PREPAID CREDIT CARD**
- **NEVER USE CORRECT INFORMATION**

- **USE DIFFERENT ONLINE SERVICES TO BUILD YOUR SITES**
- **DO NOT PUT ALL WEBSITES IN SAME ACCOUNT**

Good Luck

Chapter 25
How to Deceive Like Whitey Bulger

I have always been fascinated by people who have disappeared and stayed off the radar, like the Anglin Brothers who escaped from Alcatraz, John Darwin who faked his death in the UK. and Moana Pozzi, the Italian porn star who some believe also faked her death. If you are looking to disappear or deceive, it is important to look backward and learn from others' mistakes.

On June 23, 2011, most Americans were introduced to the name Whitey Bulger. Just in case you were busy tweeting or Facing to notice, you may have seen the movie "The Departed," by Martin Scorsese, in which Jack Nicholson's character, Costello, was loosely inspired by Whitey Bulger. The Feds posted a photo of his moll, Catherine Elizabeth Greig, on various websites, and it took only one lucky call to send the FBI to an apartment on Third Street in Santa Monica, California. A clever pretext was constructed to lure the alleged Whitey out of the apartment. Then the last letters Whitey ever wanted to hear were yelled: "FBI!" He knew his run was over. In Whitey's apartment were over eight hundred grand in cash and an arsenal of weapons.

Whitey is far from your average criminal. He is an arch-criminal, some would say a criminal's criminal. Whitey operated with the mindset of total war: anything and everything that got in his way, he mowed down. While running the streets doing business, he was also ratting to the FBI. His handlers gave him a get-out-of-jail-free card that kept him safe and put his competition in prison. The rogue FBI agent who allowed Whitey to rack up nineteen murders now looks out a window decorated with bars.

I think what shocked many was that a serial murderer like Whitey was living such a domesticated existence with his longtime lover, as opposed to living on an island in Fiji or some remote mountain in Montana. Santa Monica is beautiful, and Whitey was within walking distance of the beach. Not too shabby. With Whitey's apprehension, many reporters contacted me, asking how a criminal on the FBI's Ten Most Wanted list stays under the radar for so long.

Exit Plan – Walk Away Plan – Exit Strategy

In warfare an exit plan or strategy exists to minimize loss, be it lives or supplies. In everyday life we think about an exit plan. In response even to the simple thought, "What do I do if I lose my job?" we plan ahead. When leaders send their troops to fight, they determine the best retreat in case they face annihilation. The attack is carefully planned: how food and water are accessed and how to create/find an escape route in case the shit hits the fan.

EXIT PLAN
THINK WITH YOUR HEAD, NOT YOUR EYES

It would benefit criminals to think a little more about the future, think with their heads, not their eyes. When you think with your eyes you see only what is in front of you, and you miss the big picture. There is a TV show called "Manhunters," which tags along with the US Marshals as they hunt down fugitives. The first place the Marshals usually check is the old neighborhood, haunts like the old girlfriend's place, Grandma's, or a past slinging partner's apartment. These criminals are just stupid. I mean, who goes back to the old neighborhood when they're on the run? I'll tell you who-- most people who escape from prison or jump bail.

TIPS FOR IDIOTS
STAY AWAY FROM YOUR BABIES' MOMMA
STAY AWAY FROM YOUR GIRLFRIENDS', SISTERS'
AND MOTHER'S PLACES
DO NOT CALL ANYONE – ESPECIALLY COLLECT

The ones who really should have exit plans do not seem to have had them, like Bernie Madoff, who scammed to the tune of fifty billion, a whole lot of zeros. Marcus Schrenker, another million-dollar scammer, took his plane for a joy ride, parachuted out and let the world think he was dead. Poor Marcus! He was busted camping with a few beers. When the whip came down on financial fraudster Samuel Israel III, he parked his car on the Bear Mountain Bridge in New York and on the windshield wrote "Suicide is painless," which is the theme song to "MASH". Did Samuel think the Feds would show up and assume he'd jumped off the bridge? What an idiot. There are dozens of these financial types that lived huge and stole huge but now are in the penitentiary.

What boggles my mind is why these finance guys didn't have an exit plan. They were stealing millions at a clip and I have no doubt they could have put five or ten million dollars in a country that has no extradition with the United States.

Extradition
Legally speaking, extradition is defined as "the official surrender of an alleged criminal by one state or nation to another having jurisdiction over the crime charged; the return of a fugitive from justice, regardless of consent, by the authorities where the fugitive is found." International

extradition is generally "in response to a demand made by the executive of one nation on/to? the executive of another nation. This procedure is generally regulated by treaties." Black's Law Dictionary, 623 (8th ed., 2004).

I did a search and located a list of countries that do not have an extradition treaty with the US. Keep in mind that laws and circumstances change, so do not rely on this list. Personally, I would hire a lawyer who specialized in extradition law if there is such. Do note, though, that the following countries grant extradition without treaties:

Afghanistan, Algeria, Andorra, Angola, Armenia, Bahrain, Bangladesh, Belarus, Bosnia and Herzegovina, Brunei, Burkina Faso, Burma, Burundi, Cambodia, Cameroon, Cape Verde, the Central African Republic, Chad, China, Comoros, Congo (Kinshasa), Congo (Brazzaville), Croatia, Djibouti, Equatorial Guinea, Eritrea, Ethiopia, Gabon, Guinea, Guinea-Bissau, Indonesia, Ivory Coast, Kazakhstan, Kosovo, Kuwait, Laos, Lebanon, Libya, Macedonia, Madagascar, Maldives, Mali, Marshall Islands, Mauritania, Micronesia, Moldova, Mongolia, Montenegro, Morocco, Mozambique, Namibia, Nepal, Niger, Oman, Qatar, Russia, Rwanda, Samoa, São Tomé & Príncipe, Saudi Arabia, Senegal, Serbia, Slovenia, Somalia, Sudan, Syria, Togo, Tunisia, Uganda, Ukraine, United Arab Emirates, Uzbekistan, Vanuatu, Vatican, Vietnam, and Yemen. I don't know about the quality of life in these places so research carefully.

I decided to include Whitey Bulger's timeline on the run and offer my thoughts on his deceptive skills. I find it important to do this because in the end it was a digital action the ended Bulger's time on the run.

Jan. 3, 1995:
Bulger, who stashed money and documents in safe deposit boxes in

the United States and abroad, clears out a safe deposit box in Clearwater, Florida.

What Whitey did right was stash money all over the world in safety deposit boxes. A recent interview I saw with one of his cronies stated that Whitey had told him to save cash for that rainy day and stash it away and never tell anyone.

WALKAWAY MONEY
CASH STASHED FOR YOUR EXIT PLAN

The main problem some face while living under the radar is how to make money to survive. Walkaway money is critical to survival on the run. If one does not have cash tucked away, they will probably have to resort to crime. Resorting to crime increases chances of being captured by fifty percent.

Jan. 14-17, 1995:
Bulger and Greig are staying in Long Island, NY, under his alias, Thomas Baxter.

When it comes to disappearing, I have opposed using fake identities because it can create a lot of problems. In the criminal world one should have several aliases with CLEAN and TESTED new identities. When I say tested, I mean that the driver's license numbers are all legitimate, and if law enforcement ran that license through their systems, it would come back good and not revoked or suspended. Whitey had an advantage over most, because I would assume that several of his new identities came from his FBI handler;

May 13, 1996:
Bulger buys four pre-paid calling cards at a store in Okemah, Oklahoma. He and Greig use them to place almost 50 calls to Massachusetts over the next two months.

This is where Whitey may have made a mistake. The prepaid phones and prepaid calling cards should have been purchased prior to going on the run. But those 7-Elevens and other types of stores all have cameras, which could have discovered the car he was traveling in and blown his whole exit plan. It is a mistake to buy all the prepaid tools in one store.

May 19 to July 7, 1996:
Bulger and Greig are back in Grand Isle, renting a house they paid for with $100 bills. They leave behind clothes and an iron that are later seized by the FBI.

Cash is king! Even using prepaid credit cards can get one busted.

July 24, 1996:
Bulger and Greig travel from Chicago to New York aboard Amtrak, using the names Mark and Carol Shapeton. Bulger obviously has several CLEAN and TESTED new identities and knows when to dump an ID. Remember, the minute a new identity is utilized, it becomes vulnerable.

Jan. 2000:
Greig is spotted at a hair salon in Fountain Valley, California, where she has her hair dyed while Bulger waits in a car parked outside. This is a huge blunder. Never go on the run with another person.

You are only as strong as the weakest link, and that weak link could turn out to be the person who turns you in. Let's be realistic. There was a time when the Mafia had a code of silence, but those days appear to be over. Even Sammy the Bull turned cheese eater.

Sept. 10, 2002:
Bulger is spotted strolling along Piccadilly Circus in London by a British businessman who had met him years earlier.

Avoid tourist attractions at all cost. It appears that Whitey had the ability to travel internationally, but he should have hung low. Wandering out in places like Piccadilly Circus, Times Square, South Beach and other popular attractions where people go on vacation increases one's exposure.

Feb. 2003:
A credible sighting of Bulger is reported in Manchester, England, according to the FBI.

Again, a credible sighting of Whitey probably burned him in the UK.

June 20, 2011:
FBI launches a new campaign to collar Bulger and Greig, advertising on daytime television programs to target women Greig's age.

This was Whitey's downfall.

The FBI released a public service announcement on Monday. It targeted Bulger's longtime girlfriend Catherine Greig, mentioning her frequent visits to beauty salons and her dental hygiene, which included monthly trips to the dentist for cleanings. Those Public Service Announcements were then put on programs that are popular among women. The FBI admits that the recent publicity produced a tip that led them to the fugitives.

THE EXIT PLAN
- **CREATE AN EXIT PLAN**
- **STASH MONEY**
- **OBTAIN SAFETY DEPOSIT BOXES**
- **CREATE NEW IDENTITIES**

- **OBTAIN PREPAID PHONES AND PREPAID CALLING CARDS**
- **PAY ONLY WITH CASH**
- **OBTAIN A SECOND BOGUS IDENTITY**
- **GO ON THE RUN ALONE**
- **AVOID TOURIST ATTRACTIONS – POPULATED AREAS**
- **ANTICIPATE YOUR DOWNFALL AND WORK TO AVOID IT**

Another important piece of advice is not to visit websites that are created or written about you. For example, don't look up www.FindFrankAhearn.com. Patrick McDermott, who faked his death a few years back, learned that lesson. A few PI's were hired by a TV show to locate him and they put together a website about McDermott and they noticed a collection of IP addresses coming from an area of Mexico. Guess who they found, Patrick McDermott.

One journalist contacted me after Osama Bin Ladin was discovered and asked what I believe Bin Laden had done right and what he did wrong while on the run. Bin Laden, like Whitey, had a lot of money at his disposal and a network of associates who helped. Bin Laden existed deep off the radar because he avoided cell phones and other technologies that could trace him to physical locations. I think the general consensus was that Bin Laden was holed up in a cave somewhere deep in Afghanistan or Pakistan. I am sure that for a long time this was the case.

All the things Bin Laden avoided essentially did him no good because it was his non-use of technology and the face-to-face with associates that got him burned. The CIA was able to identify a trusted messenger and followed him to the compound. One look at the compound, and it was evident that someone important was hiding behind its high walls.

The truth is, most people who go on the run are not pursued because it is likely they will commit another crime and be apprehended. Bernie Madoff would have been chased to the far ends of the earth, while someone else, who stole maybe five million, would not. The reason is economics and a question of how bad you are wanted. Once more, law enforcement is smart enough to know that most criminals who are living under the radar resurface for a payday. Therefore, the criminal may not get caught the first time, or the second, but the third time might not be a charm.

ON A FINAL NOTE, CHANGE YOUR HABITS!

Chapter 26
Beware of Digital Revenge

The cool part of being in the type of business I am in is that nothing ever surprises or shocks me and things very rarely offend me. I guess when you are knee-deep in people's troubles, you learn not to judge and accept the fact that good people make stupid mistakes.

Over the years I have worked with countless private investigators and even some of them get played by a client or intimate partner other than their spouse. When a private investigator client contacts me and tells me they have an awkward situation they need to talk to me about, I always find it funny. Like, You dumb ass! You're in the business and you should know better!

One day, sitting like most mornings with a cup of coffee, I receive an email that says simply, "Frank, call me, important." I make the call, and Alexis, my client, a savvy investigator with years of experience, tells me she has a serious problem.

Alexis, a married woman with a few kids, developed a relationship with an office supply salesmen. They whooped it up Miami style--big nights, big restaurant bills and big hotel bills. It all came crashing down when Alexis learned that her salesman was not really doing very well on his job and he had overbilled several clients to the tune of seventy-five thousand dollars. The owner of the company did not want to involve the police and deal with the embarrassment, so he gave the salesman the option of repaying the seventy-five thousand in thirty days or he would go to the police.

The dirty salesman worked for a company named something like FMA Supplies he set up a corporation named FMA Supply, the difference in name Supplies & Supply. He would take the real invoice from his employer and dump it and create a new invoice from his bogus company for a percentage over the actual invoice. Meaning if the real company wrote an invoice for $1500.00 he would create an invoice for $1600.00 from his bogus company.

The companies would send payments to the bogus company which was a mail drop and make them out to FMA Supply the bogus company. The dirty salesman in turn would supply payments to his company via money order or cash. The accounting office at the company thought it was really odd that several clients had begun paying with cash and money orders. There was one more major trigger, and that was the fact that they were all clients of the same salesman.

The salesman admitted his situation to Alexis, and she felt bad and wanted to help her lover out--she was head over heels. The salesman guaranteed that he could get her back the money within sixty days, when another deal he was working panned out. Alexis cashed out a fund from her marital assets and figured she would have the funds replaced without her husband ever knowing. Oh, the tangled web we weave when we don't know how to deceive!

After Alexis gave the salesman the cash, he became difficult to reach. His explanation was that he was working his ass off for his new job, which was, ironically, in the same industry, office supply sales. As the countdown to return the cash got closer and closer, he was totally in the wind, and Alexis knew she had a problem, but what to do?

She laid out the whole story to me. She even got him a

cellphone under her account, as well as co-signed an auto loan. I was shocked. This is the type of story a private-investigator usually hears from a client, not something they find themself knee-deep in. Yikes! Alexis needed that cash back before her husband discovered it was missing. Of course, I can be rather devious and figure out ideas to assist Alexis, but I was hesitant and was concerned about getting caught up in a shit storm, especially a storm where I was not going to make any money. Also, my idea probably had a hint of blackmail to it. Perhaps I told Alexis what I would do in this situation and she did it, or maybe I didn't. I will never tell.

Alexis did have the option of suing and getting a judgment against the ex-lover/salesman, and then she could have attempted to search for his assets and then levy his bank account. Oh wait--not an option to search for bank accounts since the Feds passed a law a few years back--the Gramm–Leach–Bliley Act (GLB), also known as the Financial Services Modernization Act of 1999. This law prohibits a person from pretexting banks or posing as a bank employee.

Prior to 1999 I would have picked up the phone and hit up the banks with a real cool pretext of "Hi, this is Michael Christopher from Bookkeeping our systems are down, and I need you to check to see if a customer has a current account." Once we locate the account it would attach it with a lien--but no can do. Therefore, Alexis needed to come up with an alternate remedy.

If I were in her situation, I would build a website using the salesman's name, like Kyledowling.net, and since I owned the phone he was using, I would post all of the phone numbers he had called on the website, and, for the coup de grace, I would post all the emails he had sent admitting to stealing the money and having to repay the boss. I would have suggested that she claim she was going to publish the website for all to see if he did not pay the money back immediately.

Alexis was repaid without having to publish the website, it was built and he got a text message on his phone from a prepaid phone that suggested he visit www.kyledowling.net. Sometimes some digital persuasion can be useful. One needs to be careful, however, because something you do online may not seem to be a crime, but you could be wrong.

To flip this situation, you could find yourself dead smack on the receiving end of someone's digital revenge. Think about it. You may be in love now, but in six months the dirty text, the half-naked photo or the cell phone video just might be the weapon used against you and shared with your employer. Imagine the surprise on your bosses face seeing you in the buff.

From the Land Down Under, a seventeen-year-old girl got revenge on some professional sports players who had allegedly wronged her. She claimed that she and two players did the big nasty and she got pregnant and had a miscarriage. This audacious Aussie went to town and used every possible digital medium that existed to broadcast her story and take revenge. She had naked photos to share, and share she did. The footballers claimed that she had somehow obtained them illegally. Maybe she did, but it doesn't matter, since no one will ever know the truth.

Over in the UK, we move to a radio host who told a female guest who was a model that he would leave his wife and two kids to be with her. His wife, not happy on hearing the comment, decided she had had enough and took some revenge.

The wife placed an item for sale on her eBay store: "I need to get rid of this car immediately--ideally in the next 2-3 hours before my jerk husband gets home to find it gone and all his belonging's in the street." It turns out that she was the registered owner of their car, which was a Lotus Esprit. In five minutes she had sold the forty-five-thousand-dollar car for 90 cents. Ouch, that hurts!

Chapter 27
Photo Distortion & Photo Doubles

There are two tools to battle photos online. One, Photo Distortion, is the act of putting up strangers' photos and tagging them with your name. Photo Doubles is the act of putting up a photo of a stranger that purports to be you. The difference is Photo Distortion is applying your name to all different photos not claiming to be you. Photo Doubles are photos not of you claiming to be you.

Photo Distortion comes in quite handy when it comes to digital deception. If you travel a lot or are in a business that is risky, post bogus photos and let the searcher try to figure out who the real you happens to be. Then you can totally fuck with the searcher by using a Photo Double to assume your online identity. The plan here is to flood the Internet with photos of the distortion and of the double. Both of these tools are great when it comes to protecting your kid's online identity.

In my days of hunting people down, a good source was online images. Images in search engines do not necessarily compete with the same volume as information in search engines. I could search a name like Frank M. Ahearn and find a slew of pages about me and others who share the name. However, when I search images, it reduces the amount of information about me and brings up photos of others who share my name. Therefore searching images brings you less of the most popular information that is on the information search page.

What I have done is use the people, places and things

category. With people I post photos of individuals of all races and tag the client's name. I post these photos on the Fake Digital Identity websites and the Digital Distortion websites I have built. The place photos are of cities, beaches and other places/venues /locations I select, and I tag the photos "Frank M. Ahearn, Paris" or "Frank M. Ahearn, Bronx." With the things category, I have a boatload of fun by posting pictures of fried chicken, boats, snakes and bottles of beer, all tagged with "Frank M. Ahearn." The goal is to murk up searchers' results and put them in a position where they must try to figure out which photo is me/you and why all the other oddities are there.

There really isn't much to explain about Photo Distortion or Photo Doubles. Post Photos of others that are tagged with your name, or post photos that are going to assume your online identity. In the links section there are dozens of sites where you can build websites for free.

POST-POST-POST-POST-POST

Chapter 28
How to Disappear... Alcatraz Style

In my other book How to Disappear I wanted to include this story of the Anglin brothers who escaped Alcatraz but the publisher did not see how it was relevant. What a dick head considering this is one of the greatest disappearances of all time.

Speaking of the greatest disappearance and amazing act of deception two brothers from a small town in Florida, Clarence and JW Anglin are kings, who escaped from Alcatraz. I include this story because no one knows if these two made it out of the water dead or alive. Either way, they earned some ink in my book.

I met with some Hollywood producers about creating a show titled "Missing," about me finding people who have disappeared. The producers were interested in doing cases where it was possible that the missing people might still be alive, like Whitey Bulger, leader of the Winter Hill Gang; D.B. Cooper, skyjacker and bank robber; Lord Lucan, member of British high society and suspected murderer, and Moana Pozzi, Italian porn star. Out of all the cases that were kicked around, they were interested in the Anglin brothers' famed escape from Alcatraz, made popular by Clint Eastwood in his portrayal of Frank Lee Morris, one of the escapees. By the way Frank Lee Morris is not the master mind the Eastwood movie makes him out to be. My attitude about searching for the two brothers was pretty negative. I figured there was no way the Anglins or Morris made it out of the dark waters with their makeshift rafts.

I started my search by locating family. The name Anglin is a somewhat common Southern name. Most searches online brought me to IMDB.com, the movie site, that linked the movie "Escape from Alcatraz." I located an old book titled Riddle of the Rock, by Don Denevi, an interesting work that discusses the escape in detail--unlike the movie, which simplified the breakout.

The theory is that Bumpy Johnson, a notorious Harlem mob boss, assisted in the escape by having a boat waiting out in the Bay for the escapees. However, when I did my research on Bumpy Johnson, I found that he had no power left and no money to finance such a feat. In addition, relations were hostile among the different ethnic groups on the Rock, though some believe that the escape plan united the groups, who kept it a secret from the guards.

The vital hope among the prisoners was that, if the escapees made it out alive, they perhaps would shine light on the horrible conditions in Alcatraz, where, although the Warden allowed painting on canvas, The Big House was filled with small cells, no exercise and high carbohydrate diets to keep the inmates lazy. Nor were they allowed any forms of currency. Alcatraz was no Ritz Carlton

After days of spinning my skip tracing wheels, I was unsuccessful at locating any Anglin family members. Sometimes when one skip traces, the simple things are forgotten. I finally hit www.ancestry.com and started posting that I was a writer searching for Anglin family members. A few days later, I got an email from a woman who knew the oldest brother and patriarch of the family. I will refer to him as Man, a family nickname.

I dialed Man's cell phone number and an easy-going Southern

voice answered. I told him my story, that I was working with some producers who wanted to do a TV show about his brothers. Of course, I left out the part that we were looking to capture them. Man agreed to meet me at a nearby Arby's restaurant the following day.

The next day I arrived at the Arby's about forty minutes early, checking out the scene. I wasn't sure what to expect from Man or other family members. When you're a skip tracer, being paranoid at times is your best tool. The paranoia can keep you one step ahead. After assessing that all was cool, I walked into the Arby's and took a seat in a booth by the window, watching all who arrived. Shortly after, the kindest-looking person I ever met walks in, Man, brother of JW and Clarence the masters of the great escape.

As Man was sitting down, he asked if I was going to make him rich and famous. I laughed. However, Man was not joking. He told me how the media had pretty much used him and spit him out. He told me that everyone else had made money off his brothers' infamy, but the Anglin family never "received a dime from books, TV shows or movies made." My answer was simple, "How 'bout we start with a cup of coffee? I'm buying." Man smiled. He preferred bottled water.

I wanted to know about the brothers, how they found themselves in a place like Alcatraz. Clarence and JW robbed a bank in Alabama. What most people do not realize is that a third brother, Alfred Anglin, was with them, and was the supposed ringleader. Man told me that Alfred was always in trouble, and prior to the robbery in Alabama, he had been on the lam for several years, living in the middle of Florida working on a farm picking fruit and vegetables.

While hiding out in Florida, Alfred fell in love with a sixteen-year-old beauty named Jeanette. Like Romeo and Juliet's, theirs was a forbidden love. The couple crossed the state line and married.

Eventually I discovered a small graveyard with Alfred's headstone and an old photo of Alfred and Jeanette announcing their marriage for all to see, quite brazen for a man on the run. That was just the way Alfred was: he feared nothing and wanted to give his new bride more in life so he devised a plan.

While Alfred was picking fruit under the hot Florida sun, Clarence was working on a road gang somewhere around Fort Myers. Turns out Clarence's mother, Rachel, and another of her sons went to visit Clarence in jail. Clarence told them not to come the next week that he would be visiting them at home. The mother and brother shrugged it off as Clarence's usual banter.

The following week, Clarence, true to his word, escaped from the road gang with two other prisoners. Barefoot, he made his way up the Gulf Coast, wading and swimming for more than sixty miles.

Man told me that Clarence and JW were thick as thieves, and since childhood, they had had a unique way of communicating with each other about a secret meeting place: phone calls with a certain number of hang-ups determined locations. JW received such a message and met Clarence when he escaped from the Florida road gang and took him to stay with Alfred on the farm. Farm life was no life for Clarence: he had a tough edge to him and preferred easy money as opposed to a weekly paycheck. Also, picking fruit never paid that much.

The plan, Man told me, was that originally, Clarence and Alfred were going to rob the bank in Alabama, and originally JW wanted no part in the crime. JW was a ladies' man, dressed sharp and loved fast cars. A fast car was needed for the bank robbery, but JW refused to lend his car, but he eventually decided that he would go along and drive the getaway car. What the brothers did not know was that Alabama still had the death penalty for bank robbery.

My meetings with Man became weekly, kind of a Tuesdays with Morrie, but in an Arby's with me sipping bad coffee and him the usual water. Man was always cautious about how he answered my questions; in his late seventies, he was sharp. One time he was bold and told me he had to watch what he said, as he didn't want to get into any type of trouble. Not sure what he meant, I pushed on, but his big Southern smile always brought the conversation to another topic.

At another meeting with me, Man implied that I might be a US Marshal trying to capture his brothers and wanted to know if I was wired. I told him I was not. He asked me to take off my shirt and prove it to him. That afternoon in the Arby's I stood and took off my shirt as the patrons looked at me as if I was crazy.

To explain, Man pulled out the business card of a US Marshal. Forty years after the escape, the US Marshals had actually approached him and asked him to take a polygraph test. They picked him up from the small lot where he and a few siblings lived in trailers, and the Marshal drove him to an office, asked him thirteen questions, drove him back home, and never discussed the results of the test.

During the bank robbery, JW drove his brother up to the bank door. Clarence and Alfred entered the bank using a toy gun and a woman nearly fainted. The two brothers stopped the robbery and gave her a glass of water, but eventually stole about 19K. Soon the brothers are apprehended in Ohio. Less than $600 of the loot was spent. All three brothers were found guilty. Since Alfred owed the state of Georgia time for his prior escape, Alfred was sent back to Atlanta. JW and Clarence went to Leavenworth and eventually to Alcatraz because of a foiled escape in a bread box.

Fast forward to Alcatraz, June 11, 1962, Allen West, the mastermind behind the Alcatraz escape, is unable to exit his cell. JW, Clarence and Frank Lee Morris escape into the dark waters, supposedly never to be seen again.

After the escape, Man told me that while he was visiting Alfred in the penitentiary, in the prison bathroom Alfred said he had received a message from Clarence and that he knew where the brothers were holed up and was going to break out and meet up with the pair. True to his word, Alfred attempted to escape, only to be killed by electrocution by the prison fence.

Long after the Alcatraz escape, there were several sightings and assumed correspondence with JW and Clarence. By Hollywood standards, the smoking gun was a postcard that arrived in the mail to the family home from Brazil, written in Clarence's writing. Every year on their mother's birthday, she received two dozen red roses with unsigned cards. The roses stopped upon her death.

At times Man would open up and bring me closer to a world he shared with no one, not even his own siblings. The family joked about the brothers, saying that if anyone knew their whereabouts, it would be Man. I asked to see the postcard from Brazil; however, a week later Man told me the card was gone and no one could find it. I offered him twenty thousand dollars just to look at the mysterious correspondence. Man smiled and said again in that polite Southern voice that it had been misplaced.

Some years ago, "Unsolved Mysteries TV Show" did a segment about the Anglin brothers; I had the good fortune of meeting the Michael Scott the director of that segment, who was now one of the producers I was working with. We flew together to meet the US Marshal who had worked the tips from "Unsolved Mysteries."

1. A woman called in claiming to have met Clarence Anglin at a barbecue after the escape. She claimed he was with a teenage girl named Rachel. Strangely enough, as mentioned, that was the name of the Anglins' mother. The woman claimed that she had also visited the home of Clarence in Georgia and mentioned particular features about Clarence that would only have been recognized in person.

2. In the same area of Georgia, a bank was robbed, and the MO was similar to that of the Anglin bank robbery in Alabama. What's so interesting is that the Georgia bank robbery was in the same town that the Anglins hail from. Mike, the producer, told me when he was shooting the "Unsolved Mysteries" segment, he had the wanted posters of Clarence and JW faxed to a hotel manager's office in that town, and the manager remarked that one of the faces looked like that of the guy who had robbed the bank a few years back in Georgia.

3. The US Marshal met with another woman who claimed she was on her father's ranch in Texas when several men showed up who were assisting a man being smuggled into Mexico. Her father claimed it was one of the Anglin brothers.

4. We learned that only a few years back the US Marshals received a tip that one of the Anglin brothers was in Brazil. The Marshals went down to Brazil and got a confirmation from a local bartender that one of the brothers had been there. Eventually the trail went cold.

Mike and I eventually went to meet Man but first stopped in a local diner. We started talking with a few locals, one specifically who knew the family well. He told us that what most people do not know is that one of the Anglin siblings was out in California during the escape and not far from the Rock--information supposedly not in the FBI file.

The FBI file is an interesting piece of work. The attitude is summed up that most likely the trio drowned in the bay. Across the bay was a community of people known as the Colony. These were family members of inmates locked up in Alcatraz. There is no record of the FBI ever speaking to members of the Colony.

We picked up Man, who gave us a grand tour of where the Anglins grew up, from backwoods swimming holes to back roads where JW raced his Thunderbird. Man told stories of JW being a ladies' man, dressing like a fancy preacher, Clarence being tough as nails and Alfred too, well, they were both destined for trouble. Mike and I were hoping to get that smoking gun post card, but it never came.

Either way, Hollywood passed on my show titled "Missing." To them there was no smoking gun. The secret of Clarence and JW still hides behind the kind smile of a gentle old guy named Man. Through my search, I learned of things that are best left unsaid, things that imply or point to the strong possibility of life after Alcatraz for JW and Clarence.

To me it was a great experience to dive so deep into the world of such a mystery --which will never be solved, or at least not yet. That was the last time I saw Man the brother of JW, Clarence and Alfred. And that's how you disappear, Alcatraz style.

Chapter 29
To App or Not to App

No one truly knows the future of technology or how this digital revolution will actually change our lives. In simple forms we see how it has changed communications around the world and made it a smaller planet. We always have access to boundless information at our fingertips. We can buy what we want, when we want, where we want. Riding the subway this morning, I stood against the car doors as the rattling of wheels and rail shook me from a daydream. I looked at everyone in the car, some sitting, some standing, and did not see faces. I saw the tops of heads with fingers moving as fast as Jerry Lee Lewis banging out "Great Balls of Fire."

When I used to ride the subway, I was able to view a sea of information by means of who was reading what. The New York Times would offer me the world headlines, the New York Post and Daily News would compete for the most clever or cheesy of headlines. I would scan the train car for book titles people were reading, and sometime during my bookstore visits see what those books were about. But now I see only the tops of people's heads.

I usually exit at the Forty-second Street station at New York's Time Square, and it is a bombardment of digital TV screens hawking the latest and greatest advertisements. At night, Times Square is lit up like a football stadium, and for blocks you can see the glow.

My next stop is Starbucks for a latte, and there, too, most people waiting in line have heads down and fingers dancing on some type of device. Then it happened: a woman slid her IPhone under the scanner which received the payment for her drink. Shit! I used to warn people of the dangers of those discount cards and customer loyalty cards, and now the enemy, Big Business, is convincing society to put an app (software application) on their cell phones to replace the very plastic card itself.

It was bad enough that the loyalty card was tracing your purchases. Now some card are stand-alone, that is, they do not have an identifier attached to them, while others are associated with an email address. I decided to check out the app, and when I went to download it, it wanted full Internet access to my phone, my Coarse network-based locations, and my Fine (GPS) location. I had no clue what these words meant, nor was there a brief explanation offered for a techno-dope such as myself.

I headed over to the website of the app creator and read that he was a third party not associated with Starbucks. Let me tell you that again--a third party not associated with Starbucks. The developer created the application in January 2011, and in February 2011 was served a "cease and desist" letter by Starbucks asking him to stop using the Starbucks name and logo. Using my nifty skip tracing abilities, I checked the WHOIS on the website and found that the actual website was created in December 2011. The WHOIS has a name and address for the registrant but no phone number or email contact. As of this writing, the app has had over fifty thousand downloads.

The moral of the story is you are giving access to someone that may have connection to the company the app represents.

I contacted the app's developer, posing as a student doing a project about apps--digital undercover, you could say--and I asked the following questions:

1. Does a developer like you make money when people download or use the app?

2. Why do apps need both Coarse (network-based) locations and a? Fine (GPS) location?

3. Do third party companies collect or store information when the app is used?

There was no response from the company to my questions.

The real question here is, what information do the third party App companies have access to on our phones? Forget a phone virus, and maybe wiping out our information. Can they access our phone book, email contacts, dirty text messages to our other half? Maybe they can record our passwords or phone history. Several of the various app companies I researched do not list on the download or their website what they actually have access to on your phone. It's a mystery without any clues.

This app journey took me to the next step: can apps or software spy on you and your phone? Obviously a dumb question posed by? Frank M. Ahearn. The answer is yes. Check out items available from Mobile Spy.

Mobile Spy is the next generation of smartphone spy software. Do you suspect your child or employee is abusing his SMS or vehicle privileges? If so, then this software is ideal for you. Install this small program directly onto the compatible smartphone you wish to monitor, and it will begin recording.

Using the Internet capabilities of your phone, you can quickly upload recorded activities, logs and GPS locations to your Mobile Spy account. To view the results, you simply log in to your secure account at the Mobile Spy website. Logs are displayed by categories and sorted for easy browsing.

For a small fee you will also be able to see the phone's screen and location on a map LIVE. You can then view phone info instantly and remotely control the device. The add-on also allows you to have your logs emailed to you.

The software is completely stealthy? and works independently. Mobile Spy does not rely on the phone's call and message logs to record activities. So even if the user tries to delete his tracks, the data will still be retained and uploaded. Mobile Spy is compatible with most models of iPhone, BlackBerry or Android phones! And it is also compatible with Windows Mobile, Symbian OS and iPad.

From Mobistealth - Catch Cheating Spouse with Mobile Spy Software

Mobistealth Spy software for iPhone, BlackBerry and Android phones is a must-have mobile Spy a?/App to expose all secrets. If you are a spouse who suspects your partner might be having an affair, want to find out if he/she is telling the truth, or have a need to discover details of the affair, then MobiStealth Spy Software for Cell Phones is the perfect solution for you.

Listen to Calls
Listen to Voices in Surroundings
Read SMS Messages
View Call History and Contacts
Track Location, and much more...

Some of the software available can work as a bug and record conversation while the spied-upon victim is not on the phone. This means the software can pick up non-telephone/surrounding conversation wherever the victim is sitting, standing, eating or enjoying an evening spritz at the spa. Most of the companies that provide the software claim it is untraceable.

At the moment the only plus for the phone owner is that the person attempting to place the spyware on your phone needs to physically download it directly to your phone. The only way to protect yourself is never to let your phone out of your sight. It wouldn't hurt to put a mark on your phone, too, in case your actual phone is switched by a mate. Also, be cautious if someone gives you a new phone; it could be a compromised unit.

I wouldn't be surprised if some time in the near future an App will be made for spyware. To App or not to App – Mobi be the question! - I know that's a cheesy statement but I could not help it

Chapter 30
Rules of the Game

In my days of skip tracing and extracting people's personal information, I was very cautious and had a set of rules I always abided by. If I had a bad feeling or an uncomfortable feeling about a client, I would not do business with them. If I was planning to extract information and became suspicious of the integrity of the work, I would take a pass. If I felt there was too big a risk and that obtaining the information would kick back on me, I would also pass. Sometimes clients would offer me huge amounts of money to do crazy things or extract extremely sensitive information, and I would decide if it was worthwhile by asking the client if they would pay for my legal fees if I got caught. If they said no, it was, "Adios, dude. I am not doing the work."

We are facing a future where privacy is dwindling extremely fast, and not too far off in the future, there will be no public privacy. Soon cameras will exist everywhere in public. If you have an appointment, the minute you leave your apartment, it is most likely that your building will has a camera in the lobby. If you take public transportation, the bus or train could have a camera. The intersections you traverse have cameras. If you decide to stop in a store and buy a soda, there will be a camera at the cash register. When you walk into an office building, you need to show identification and they take your photo. Then you enter the elevator, where there is also a camera. Finally, the office you visit might have a camera, too. That is a lot of cameras, and it's only the introduction to our future of digital control.

Check out this company--GeoTime (www.geotime.com)--and really take a look at the type of software it has created.

GeoTime creates some serious James Bond shit, and it's all about being able to identify our movements and our connections. Sure, it's a crime fighting but the bottom line is that it's all about the ability to track people and their movements. We find these types of things on our current phone, with apps requesting access to our locations. We are going to see a rapid growth in this type of public tracking for private financial gain.

In different parts of the world, there have been small acts of rebellion against street cameras. In the UK a small town installed a street camera where the teens tend to hang out. What the teens began doing was all wearing jeans and the same color hoodie sweatshirts and walking around with the hoods up and faces down. If some teen shit happened, the police would not be able to identify the culprit.

And in parts of France, drivers began vandalizing traffic cameras by covering them with plaster of Paris. In some US town, a guy took a photo of the mayor's car's license plate and blew it up and placed it over his own license plate and began blowing red lights, which sent tickets directly to the mayor. To me, this is the human spirit speaking!

You cannot stop what will soon be happening in terms of surveillance in the streets of every city in the world. However, you can embrace your own form of rebellion like those I've shared with you.

Combating the digital future is all about mindset and imposing some digital self-values. You do control a certain amount of information that flows online, and that is the information you should be taking down from the public eye. I personally find it surprising that Americans have run hypnotized to the land of social networking without any real forethought about what they are participating in, like lemmings walking off a cliff. I do not mean that as an insult, but this is supposed to be the land of freedom and democracy, but all of this putting your information online and being a part of it seems more communistic than independent in spirit.

At this very moment there is some squint, geek or techie out there trying to figure out how to use your information and entice you to become a member of his/her new social sites for the sole purpose of his becoming the next Mark Zuckerberg.

SOME RULES OF THE GAME
CELL PHONE RULES
DO NOT TAKE COMPROMISING PHOTOS
DO NOT STORE COMPROMISING PHOTOS
DO NOT SEND COMPROMISING TEXT MESSAGES
DO NOT SEND COMPROMISING EMAILS
ALL ACTIONS ARE AVAILABLE TO HACKERS AND LAW ENFORCEMENT

I've already written about the perils of cell phones and the hacking that has taken place. There will be no surprises in the future when more celebrities' cell phones are hacked. It's a simple concept: if it is on your cell, it is available for the entire world to see.

ONLINE RULES
JUST BECAUSE THEY ASK, DOES NOT MEAN YOU NEED TO TELL THE TRUTH
DO NOT POST CORRECT INFORMATION
DO NOT POST PHOTOS

It is a simple concept: if you post something online once, it has the ability to evolve into a million pages or hits. Your private photos, thoughts and transgressions can become fodder for others' entertainment.

IN PUBLIC
ASSUME AND ACCEPT THAT EVERYTHING IN PUBLIC IS RECORDED, NO IFS, ANDS, OR BUTS

In the UK a few months back, a guy came home and could not find his cat. He had a cam set up outside his door and began to review the day's happenings. What he discovered was real fucked-up: a woman had passed by his front stoop, picked up his cat and thrown it into a garbage can. She placed the lid on the can and walked off. He called the police and posted the video online, and it went viral. It was only a matter of hours before she was identified and then pegged as the most hated woman in the UK.

Chapter 31
New Identities

In my last book, *How to Disappear*, I was reluctant to write about how one would obtain a new identity since the book was geared to individuals with legitimate problems. I searched the Internet and reviewed how others suggest going about obtaining a new identity. So consider this the Frank M. Ahearn critique of new identity suggestions.

Grave Robbing
In the past grave robbing was probably the most common way individuals obtained new identities. You would cruise cemeteries and find a child who had died before the age of five and who was born roughly around your year of birth. The idea was that once you had located your subject, you would search the background information on the family of the deceased and go to the county office and obtain a birth certificate.

Nowadays, when obtaining a birth certificate, generally a Social Security number is required on the application. Some individuals who stated they'd obtained a new identity claimed that they lived outside of the country and are now returning to the US to reestablish themselves. That may have worked in the seventies in Mayberry RFD, but it would never fly now, especially not in a large city. It definitely will not work in today's digital world. In order to obtain a copy of a birth certificate today, you need to provide City Clerks with one type of acceptable identification below:

Types of Acceptable Identification
Driver's license

Non-driver's license
Passport
Naturalization Papers
Military ID
Employer's Photo ID
Two utility bills showing the applicant's name and address
Police report of lost or stolen ID

Unless you have one of these acceptable forms of identification, you are not getting a copy another person birth certificate of the deceased.

In the skip tracing world there is also the fluke factor, which is that thing that has nothing to do with anything that blows your plan out of the water. For instance, imagine you send in the application and an employee in the office just happens to know the family of the deceased.

War Buddy
Another way to obtain a new identity is the war buddy plan. If you just happened to be in the military during a time of war, this might be the route to take. If you know the name of someone killed or missing in action, try to obtain his or her identity/birth certificate?. The problem with this plan is that everyone who enters the military has a Social Security number, and if they are killed, their death/number is reported to Social Security and the Department of Vital Statistics.

As far as the missing-in-action scenario is concerned, I tried to search what happens if a member of the forces goes missing and what happens to their benefits. Unfortunately, I was unable to locate an answer. Either way, this method just does not seem viable.

One Website Suggests
There are a lot of logical reasons for a person not to get a Social

*Security number until late in life. You may claim that you are ...
A person just released from an institution, like a prison or a mental
hospital, may never have had a card. Someone who's been a
"perpetual student," spending years accumulating degrees, may not
have one. The best ruse is most likely that you've been living abroad
since your parents moved to Canada when you were a teenager. Any
of these ruses should be enough to bore the clerk into issuing the
number.*

Whoever wrote this is freaking moron! I checked to see if
inmates are issued Social Security numbers upon entering the
system but could not locate an answer, but I am sure they are.
Also, walking into a Social Security office and explaining that
you were released from prison and have no Social Security
could be a risky venture as well as a red flag to the person
assisting you. Also you are not going to bore someone into
issuing a social security number.

Baptismal Certificates
Recently I had to obtain my baptismal certificate, and when I
called I was asked quite a few questions over the phone: my
parents' names and dates of birth, my mother's maiden name
and my full name and date of birth.

Forging Documents
One site I came across suggested that you falsify your
documents.

*To forge a birth certificate is just a matter of taking a real one and
altering it. This can be done by copying it in a photocopy machine,
taking the copy, blanking out the filled-in spaces, recopying it]. Once
you have done this, you can fill in the blanks, recopy it and you're in
business.*

This idiot forgot to mention that when you are attempting to
obtain various types of identification, an original birth

certificate with a SEAL is needed for the applications, not copies. I tested my own birth certificate. I made a copy and the word VOID is all over the copied version. They also forget to mention the fact that birth certificates have a registration number assigned.

After much reading about obtaining new identities online, I came to realize that the information offered on most websites and books is just a bunch of bullshit! Truthfully, if you follow the methods offered online, you will most likely end up in jail.

Some websites offer a new driver's license, which eventually comes in the mail and is a go-cart license or some other type of silly document. Some websites sell new birth certificates, which come from non-existing countries like Mancoco.

New Numbers for Domestic Violence Victims

People in all walks of life can be victims of family violence, harassment, abuse or life-endangering situations. If you are a victim of family violence, Social Security may be able to help you. Although Social Security does not routinely assign new numbers, they will do so when evidence shows you are being harassed or abused or your life is endangered.

Applying for a new number is a big decision. It may impact your ability to interact with federal and state agencies, employers and others. This is because your financial, medical, employment and other records will be under your former Social Security number and name (if you change your name). If you expect to change your name, they recommend that you do so before applying for a new number. There are three things to know about Social Security cards:

To apply for an original card, you must provide at least two documents to prove age, identity, and US citizenship or current lawful work-authorized immigration status. If you are not a US citizen and do not have Department of Homeland Security work authorization, you must prove that you have a valid non-work reason for requesting a card.

To apply for a replacement card, you must provide one document to prove your identity. If you were born outside the US, you must also provide documents to prove your US citizenship or current lawful work-authorized status

Public Law 108-458 limits the number of replacement Social Security cards you may receive to three per calendar year and ten in a lifetime. Cards issued to reflect changes in your legal name or changes to a work authorization do not count toward these limits. They may also grant exceptions to these limits if you provide evidence from an official source to establish that a Social Security card is required.

Evidence of Documents
The following are types of documents you must provide with your application. But they are not all-inclusive:

Evidence of Age
In general, you must provide your birth certificate. In some situations, they may accept another document that shows your age, including a US hospital record of your birth (created at the time of birth) or a religious record established before age five showing your age or date of birth.

Evidence of Identity
You must provide current unexpired evidence of identity in your legal name, which will be shown on the Social Security

card. Generally, they prefer to see documents issued in the US. Documents you submit to establish identity must show your legal name AND provide biographical information (your date of birth, age, or parents' names) and/or physical information (photograph or physical description--height, eye and hair color, etc.). If you send a photo identity document but do not appear in person, the document must show your biographical information (e.g., your date of birth, age, or parents' names). Generally, documents without an expiration date should have been issued within the past two years for adults and within the past four years for children.

As proof of your identity, you must provide a US driver's license, a US state-issued non-driver's identity card, or a US passport.

If you do not have one of the documents or cannot get a replacement within ten work days, they may accept other documents that show your legal name and biographical information, such as a US military identity card, Certificate of Naturalization, employee identity card, certified copy of a medical record (clinic, doctor or hospital), health insurance card, Medicaid card, or school identity card/record. For young children, they may accept medical records maintained by a medical provider (clinic, doctor, or hospital). They may also accept a final adoption decree, a school identity card, or another record maintained by a school.

Evidence of US Citizenship
Normally, you must provide your US birth certificate or US Passport. Other documents you may have to provide are a Consular Report of Birth, Certificate of Citizenship, or Certificate of Naturalization.

Evidence of Immigration Status
After reading all of this information provided by Social

Security, it is safe to assume it is no walk in the park trying to get a new Social Security number or card. I think this also precludes the idea of "becoming" your war buddy or a deceased child. Before you attempt to obtain a new identity, you need to take into consideration the penalties involved. No matter how you slice it, if caught, you will most likely end up being charged with identity theft.

The Identity Theft Penalty Enhancement Act was created to for punishment for identity theft. This federal law prescribes various prison terms and mandatory penalties for persons who use identity theft to commit various crimes like mail fraud and terrorism. This law specifically establishes in the Federal criminal court the offense of aggravated identity theft, which is the use of stolen identity to commit crimes.

When someone is convicted of mail fraud using stolen personal information, two sentences can be imposed, one for mail fraud and one for aggravated identity theft. Those convicted of aggravated identity theft must serve an additional mandatory two-year prison term. Terrorism-related convictions using identity theft impose an additional prison sentence of five years. In addition, those convicted of aggravated identity theft may not serve their sentence on probation.

Aggravated identity theft and identity theft used even to support terrorism can lead to penalties and prison terms. In other words, direct involvement in terrorism is not necessary; the mere support of it using identity theft is sufficient to send you to jail. One example is supplying fake passports and IDs using other people's identities. Ouch! All the websites out there offering information about obtaining a new identity forget to mention and share the potential penalties.

Buying a New Identity

Early on in my skip tracing days, there was a skip tracer who bought information from a Social Security employee. What he did was drive to a Social Security building and sit in surveillance and locate an employee who had a really crappy car. He did some reconnaissance on the individual and learned that his house and personal life were as crappy as the car he drove.

One day after work the skip tracer met up with this man in a bar and developed a drinking relationship. After a few weeks the skip tracer laid his cards on the table, explaining that he could sell Social Security information for a good price. The employee agreed and so they prospered, the skip tracer getting all the information he needed and making money hand over fist, until they both got popped. The employee ultimately freaked and turned himself in to his boss, which led to the downfall of the skip tracer. The moral of the story: two people cannot keep a secret, and the person who sold you the new identity just might turn you in if they need a get-out-of-jail-free card.

If you are going the route of buying that new identity in a dark alley, there are some things to consider: Is that identity one of ten? Meaning, Will nine other people be walking around with the name Ted Smith? If so, the day you get pulled over or walk through customs, you'd better have the name of a good lawyer.

If I had a buck for every email that inquired about obtaining new identities, I would be sitting on the banks of the River Seine sipping a latte right now. The idea of new identities is fool's gold, and any person or book that tells you differently is merely selling you the fable of the Emperor's New Clothes —- you might believe there is truth and substance to what others say, but you're just naked underneath.

There are a few ways one can obtain a new identity. The first route is buying, the second is stealing, and the third is creating. All of them are illegal and can land you in the Graybar Hotel for a year or two.

But let's say you want to buy a new identity. Other than emailing me, where do you really go to buy one? Craigslist or some other type of message board, sorry, but a cop is probably sitting at the end of that email address. Maybe you have a friend who knows a guy who knows another guy, but those things are usually dead ends.

Even if you happen to stumble onto someone who claims they can get you a new identity, the key question is, How do you confirm that the driver's license, Social Security number or passport number is valid, meaning actually the correct name for the identification. And what if that guy who sold the same identity to ten people?

The next route is stealing another person's identity. However, that's just a crash and burn. As much as we hear about stolen identities, it is not really an easy feat to accomplish. Also, you never know about the secrets in the closet of the person whose identity you steal. He could be someone on a watch-list or on parole, who knows but too many unknown factors.

The final route is to create your own identity. From what I have figured, you need three separate identities to exist successfully as another person. The first identity is the "I" identity, to be used for identification purposes, while the second, the "A" identity, is used for assets. The third, the "M" identity, is used for moving on in case you need to hit the road. Only a fool would decide to disappear and have only one identity. What would happen if that identity was blown? My idea is that the three separate identities should never cross paths or be connected.

The "I" identity is what's in your wallet. It is your walk-around identity and the name everyone knows you by. You have no actual banking or credit cards under this name; you use only prepaid credit cards that do NOT require a Social Security number, or you use only cash. You should never apply under this identity for anything that requires a credit check or identifier to be used with money, like a bank account. Therefore, you need to exist solely as this entity, and you should open a shelf corporation that does not make any income and use only the corporation to rent a home and obtain utilities or cable service. Or, to be super-secure, you can sublet an apartment with no lease.

The "A" identity is all assets. It is the identity that you attach to all of your money and financial matters. I suggest you keep it simple and not apply for credit cards. What is the point of risking that identity with some unknown factor? Never have the "A" identity bank statements mailed to you. Use online statements or a mail drop. This identity needs to be renewed every year.

The "M" identity is your get-out-of-Dodge identity, the one you need to use if you need to move on if one of the other identities is blown. The big question is, Where do you get these identities? What I tell mystery writers to do in their stories is to have their character volunteer in a hospital where people are either in comas or mentally ill, and use their identities. Pretty fucking cold, but that is the only route I see.

Keep in mind that the "A" identity used for income needs to be renewed every year because the people in the hospitals are on disability and if income is made and reported, there will be a flag.

All of this is illegal and will land you in prison if you attempt it and get caught. I suggest not going any of these routes. If you are not on the run, what's the point?

The End!

Final Words

"The greatest trick the Devil ever pulled was convincing the world he didn't exist." Kevin Spacey from *The Usual Suspects*

"The greatest trick the digital world has pulled is making the world believe they want to exist in the digital world." Frank M. Ahearn *The Digital Hit Man*

15564323R00085

Made in the USA
Lexington, KY
04 June 2012